# PRAYER

## AND

# THE STRUGGLE
# AGAINST EVIL

——◆——

JOHN BARTON

DANIEL LLOYD

JAMES RAMSAY

ALEXANDER RYRIE

——◆——

FAIRACRES PUBLICATIONS 190

SLG Press
Oxford

© 2021 SLG Press

First Edition 2021

Fairacres Publications No. 190

Print ISBN 978-0-7283-0313-3

Fairacres Publications Series ISSN 0307-1405

Paul Monk asserts his right under the Copyright, Designs and Patents Act 1988, to be identified as the author of the Preface of this work.
John Barton asserts his right under the Copyright, Designs and Patents Act 1988, to be identified as the author of the chapter 'Deliver us from Evil' in this work.
Daniel Lloyd asserts his right under the Copyright, Designs and Patents Act 1988, to be identified as the author of the chapter 'Recognizing Evil' in this work.
James Ramsay asserts his right under the Copyright, Designs and Patents Act 1988, to be identified as the author of the chapter 'Speak no Evil' in this work.
Alexander Ryrie asserts his right under the Copyright, Designs and Patents Act 1988, to be identified as the author of the chapter 'Prayer and the Struggle against Evil' in this work.

The publishers have no control over, or responsibility for, any third-party website referred to in this book. All internet addresses given in the this book were correct at the time of going to press. The authors and publisher regret any inconvenience caused if addresses have changed or sites have ceased to exist, but can accept no responsibility for any such changes.

Edited and typeset in Palatino Linotype by Julia Craig-McFeely

SLG Press
Convent of the Incarnation
Fairacres • Oxford
www.slgpress.co.uk

Printed by
Grosvenor Group Ltd, Loughton, Essex

# PRAYER

## AND

# THE STRUGGLE
# AGAINST EVIL

# CONTENTS

———◆———

———◆———

*Evil subsists as soon as it is chosen; it comes into being whenever we elect it. It has no substance of its own; apart from deliberate choice evil exists nowhere.*

GREGORY OF NYSSA
Sermon 5, on Mercy


*The disciple can only set out from our dark confusion towards the Beloved who calls us and longs for us; to this Beloved who longs to incorporate us into the Trinitarian relationships of wonder and love, for here alone is Truth and reality.*

REVD JAMES COUTTS
Sermon preached at Tymawr Convent, 20 November 2014

# DELIVER US FROM EVIL

## John Barton

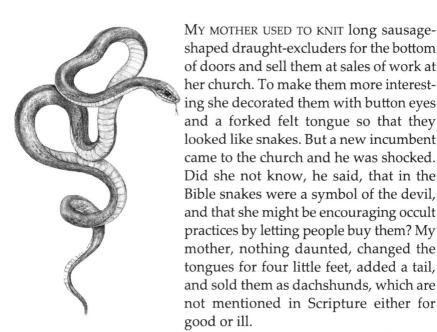

MY MOTHER USED TO KNIT long sausage-shaped draught-excluders for the bottom of doors and sell them at sales of work at her church. To make them more interesting she decorated them with button eyes and a forked felt tongue so that they looked like snakes. But a new incumbent came to the church and he was shocked. Did she not know, he said, that in the Bible snakes were a symbol of the devil, and that she might be encouraging occult practices by letting people buy them? My mother, nothing daunted, changed the tongues for four little feet, added a tail, and sold them as dachshunds, which are not mentioned in Scripture either for good or ill.

Such sensitivity as this to possible symbols of the devil is probably unusual, but the incident reminded me that there are people in the Church today who are indeed extremely aware of the devil and see his hand everywhere. At one time such an interest was perhaps a mark of a certain kind of Catholic mentality, but today it seems to have become a clear indication of a particular type of evangelicalism, as in the case of my mother's vicar. It is easy to mock when it becomes a knee-jerk reaction (and I have just done so). But evangelicals who are deeply concerned about the devil and all his works have a point when they say that this is a continual concern in the New Testament, and that the modern world is out of step with Scripture in ignoring the power and danger of the forces of evil. One of the reasons for the fame of Jesus was that He became known as an exorcist. The usual explanation of this now is to say that many things were attributed to demon-possession in the world of first-century Judaism which today we should explain biologically, but that Jesus naturally accommodated himself to the beliefs of His time; indeed He could not have failed to do so without falling out of His frame, so to speak. But we do not treat all of Jesus's teaching in this way: for example, His teaching on sexual matters and on love for one's neighbour are not given this kind of dismissal. So perhaps it will not do simply to explain away a belief in dark forces like this. The Gospels speak decisively of the existence of non-human powers in the world that may be benign or malignant; angels or devils. And we ought to give some account of that belief.

It seems to me that a belief in such powers is hardly *de fide*: I would not say that someone who did not believe in them was not a Christian, but it does seem that a great deal is lost if we do not give some place in our system of belief to forces that cannot be reduced simply to human control. Where the devil is concerned, it is open to Christians, I believe, to interpret scriptural language as referring not to a person—for surely anything we could call diabolical would have to be sub-personal, as much as God is supra-personal—but to the shapeless horror that threatens human life; the plague that stalks by night and the pestilence that destroys at noon-day, as Psalm 91 puts it.

I doubt whether that horror is mainly to be encountered in those rather marginal occult actions and practices that evangelical Christians in particular seem to get so worked up about. I do not doubt that there are people who go in for magic and witchcraft, but I do not think one meets them on every street corner, or that, for example, children who dress up as witches at Hallowe'en are endangering their souls, still less that they are doing so by reading the highly moral and wholesome Harry Potter books. It seems to me to lurk in other places altogether, and actually to be more a part of daily life, not less, than if we associate with overtly occult beliefs and doings, a point explored by James Ramsay below. The demonic is present where human life is distorted and corrupted by forces that human beings cannot control, and it is such forces from which we most need deliverance by God.

Distortion and corruption of the good for human beings occurs through economic forces that, once unleashed, cannot be tamed. It also occurs through mass hysteria and the whole mentality of large groups, in which the will of a collective mass of people overpowers the intentions of any given individual and makes all individuals mere cogs in a destructive machine. There is an illustration of this in Umberto Eco's novel *Foucault's Pendulum*, in which a group of friends invent a conspiracy theory, for their own entertainment, that goes on to acquire a life of its own as people start to believe in it: it results in death and disaster. On a much smaller scale, I recall when I was at school that a group of actors came to show us how to play a scene from Shakespeare: they chose Mark Anthony's speech after the death of Julius Caesar, with ourselves (perhaps sixty or so children) playing the crowd. We got so involved that they had to stop the play and calm us down, because the situation was turning dangerous. It would perhaps not be attempted nowadays, but in the 1960s the danger was less clearly seen. No one individual was to blame, yet the baying mob we were turning into could have done real damage. That is the kind of thing I understand by evil, and it has nothing to do with ghosts and hauntings such as those that appear in film and fiction, described by Daniel Lloyd below, but only with the dynamics of large groups.

At the individual level, evil occurs where people have the kind of dysfunctional personality that poisons everything and everyone around them. I know someone whose very presence causes strife and dissension; as soon as this person is around, people start to argue not just with them, but with each other, in highly destructive ways that threaten to spoil all the good of human friendship and solidarity. I am convinced that this individual is not to blame for this: it is a personality problem quite outside their own control. Any human community is vulnerable to such people, who are also very adversely affected themselves by the wake of desolation they leave behind them. I do not talk in such a case of 'possession'—I would use more psychiatric language, probably thinking of borderline personality disorder—but I am clear that the phenomenon is one that other times and places would identify as demonic, and correctly in so far as it is not the product of any person's deliberate sin: it seems to come from beyond the person in question. Even if the problem for this person is a psychological one, the problem for everyone else is its power to create an atmosphere in which nobody else can flourish; this power seems to have a life of its own, like the brooding sense of evil that some people can sense in a place where bad things have happened. In this it is quite like the collective madness of a crowd out of control, that does things no individual member would be likely to do of their own volition. It is in this kind of phenomenon that I would see the work of forces we would call demonic. Even if they arise out of the human psyche rather than from some malign fallen angel, they have all the characteristics that people in the time of Jesus attributed to such a source: they reduce human beings to a subhuman level. And this kind of evil is indeed all around us, not just in the fevered imagination of a certain kind of Christian but in the daily experience of everyone.

It is for this reason that we still need, as much as anyone ever did, the message that Jesus is the supreme exorcist, that is, the one who can tame the destructive powers of evil. The New Testament writers are of course unanimous in believing that Christ has indeed conquered the forces of darkness. St Paul, and the epistles attributed to him such as Colossians and Ephesians that are widely believed to be from rather later authors, speak freely of Christ as overwhelming the principalities and powers that govern the world. There are reasons in the background of early Christian belief that made this an important theme, but I have sometimes wondered whether at its root is the memory that Jesus had indeed been a great exorcist. St Paul is said to have known very little about the earthly Jesus, but perhaps he knew that much. The Cross is presented in Colossians as the place where a final victory over the forces of evil was won, and Christians were set free from the grip of the rulers of this world to take their place with Jesus in the heavenly realm. Human liberation from shapeless horror is promised through people's association with the risen and ascended Lord, who makes possible a human community free from malignant and corrupting influences.

In the light of our continuing experience of such influences, we are bound to say that if victory is essentially won, there do still seem to be some mopping-up exercises to do; but the early Christian conviction was that Christ's healing and wholesome power would in the end remove the demonic from the world. However we conceptualize evil, we continue to affirm that conviction, as we pray (in the words of the Litany) that God will 'finally beat down Satan under our feet'. The world is full of evil forces that we cannot control; as Christians we trust in the love of God, which in the end casts out fear.

It remains true that there are strange experiences of evil that do not seem to be merely the effect of malign personalities, but appear to lurk in particular places. The Anglican Church and its clergy are not best known as exorcists, but every diocese has a 'deliverance minister' who tries to deal with these experiences when they arise (usually people who have proved to be sensitive to the evidence of spiritual forces that need to be removed or laid to rest). An excellent recent introduction to the whole subject is Jason Bray's *Deliverance*.[1] He shows that priests exercising this ministry need to balance sensitivity to real evil (and lesser manifestations of disturbing activity) with common sense and a healthy scepticism, yet he remains sure that sometimes exorcism (deliverance) is appropriate, and effective.

It is important not to diagnose 'possession' where a psychiatric explanation is called for. I had a student once who was suffering from severe depression, but whose vicar diagnosed demonic possession and exorcized her, as a result of which the depression only deepened further. This was wholly misguided, and derived from the over-active imagination about the forces of evil that inspired my mother's vicar to condemn her draught-excluders. Yet there remains

---

[1] Jason Bray, *Deliverance: Everyday Investigations into Poltergeists, Ghosts and other Supernatural Phenomena by an Anglican Priest* (London: Coronet, 2021).

a residuum of cases where even down-to-earth, common-sense people become aware of malignant atmospheres, and strange events that seem to elude explanation in terms of 'natural' causes or hostile personalities. It is neither sound science nor sound theology simply to ignore or explain away such things. There is some reason why a belief in ghosts and hauntings arose in the first place, and though many accounts of them are no doubt figments of the imagination, there is a hard core where that explanation will not work. Evil is real, and takes many forms. Jesus cast out demons, and perhaps that was not merely an accommodation to the beliefs of His contemporaries, but a real expression of the goodness of God that can conquer forces beyond the human.

What, finally, we do about evil comes down to each of us: do we simply accept it as a part of life and perhaps try to avoid it, or do we engage with it and, as Alexander Ryrie says below, struggle against it?

———◆———

# RECOGNIZING EVIL
## Daniel Lloyd

In her essay, 'The Catholic Novelist in the Protestant South', Flannery O'Connor writes that 'evil is not simply a problem to be solved, but a mystery to be endured'.[1] Her life was one circumscribed by illness; her fiction is rooted in the American South, her characters idiosyncratic but fundamentally ordinary and domestic. She was born, and died, in Georgia, though she travelled across the United States (and to Lourdes) before her death at 39.[2] Though her themes are large—good, evil, grace, faith, race—her fiction is intimate, even oppressive at times. What could a perspective like this, small, if not narrow, have to say about evil? Or rather, how could evil be understood as a small thing?

Near the very beginning of his monumental work, the *Summa Theologiae*, St Thomas Aquinas discusses the existence of God.

---

[1] Flannery O'Connor, 'The Catholic Novelist in the Protestant South', in *Mystery and Manners: Occasional Prose*, ed. Robert Fitzgerald and Sally Fitzgerald (New York: Farrar, Straus, and Giroux, 1969), 209.

[2] See Brad Gooch, *Flannery: a Life of Flannery O'Connor* (London: Little, Brown, 2009).

Treating the very question, 'Does God exist?', Thomas follows his customary academic process: he raises objections that he can foresee, proposes an alternative on which he then elaborates, and concludes by answering the particular details of the objections that his imagined opponent has put to him. The objections themselves are never constructed in bad faith, never intentionally ridiculous. They are not mere straw men in the face of which Thomas can demonstrate his own learning, but very often employ biblical, patristic, or philosophical texts that, if known to an interlocutor, would quite naturally be brought out in relation to the matter under discussion. Indeed, if the objections were evidently foolish, this would rob his answers of their seriousness. It is in answering the question of the existence of God that Thomas brings to bear his famous 'Five Ways', that are treated in greater depth in others of his works, including the *Summa contra Gentiles*. There, they are described as *rationes ad probandum Deum esse*—'arguments in proof of the existence of God', and we do better if we read them as 'proving' in the sense of 'testing', rather than of incontrovertible demonstration of a fact that cannot be denied or understood other than in the way Thomas presents it. The Five Ways ensure that those with whom Thomas is discussing God know what he means by 'God'. In any case, as well known as the Five Ways are, it is in the first objection which precedes them that I am particularly interested. It runs as follows:

> It seems that God does not exist; because if one of two contraries be infinite, the other would be altogether destroyed. But the word 'God' means that He is infinite goodness. If, therefore, God existed, there would be no evil discoverable; but there is evil in the world. Therefore God does not exist.[3]

For Thomas, then, it is not unreasonable to argue that because there is 'evil discoverable', 'evil in the world', *malum in mundo*, we could therefore conclude that God does not exist. The existence of a given objection to a proposition does not mean that Thomas agrees with that objection, but it may indicate that such an objection is not

---

[3] Thomas Aquinas, *Summa Theologiae* I, Q. 2, a. 3, obj. 1.

uncommon or could be put on the basis of some writing or thought that deserves proper consideration. An atheistic response to the idea of the existence of God based on 'evil in the world' is not easy to discover in writings prior to, or contemporary with, Thomas, but he has evidently anticipated something present in the thought of David Hume and in the much more recent works of J. L. Mackie and William Rowe.[4] At this early point in the *Summa*, Thomas has neither discussed nor defined evil, but he will go on to do so in Questions 48 and 49 of the *Prima Pars*, and elsewhere throughout his writings. But the idea is already there: evil, *malum*, whatever it is, is of such significance that it could cause one to doubt God's existence. It is important to note that there is no extended treatment in Thomas's works of what would later come to be called 'the problem of evil', that we can put most simply as asking how it can be that evil and God could both be said to exist. In that light, we might conceivably be disappointed in the answer we do get to the idea that God's existence can be disproven or cast into doubt by 'evil in the world'. Thomas's reply to the objection is simply this:

> As Augustine says (*Enchiridion* xi): 'Since God is the highest good, He would not allow any evil to exist in His works, unless His omnipotence and goodness were such as to bring good even out of evil.' This is part of the infinite goodness of God, that He should allow evil to exist, and out of it produce good.[5]

The Dominican philosopher Brian Davies argues that the reason for this brisk disposal, not only of the objection itself but also (albeit in advance) of the genre of theological and philosophical writing to which the sort of idea contained in the objection has given rise is that, for Thomas, such a question is, in fact, a 'pseudo-problem':

---

[4] See, for example, J. L. Mackie, 'Evil and Omnipotence', *Mind* 64/254 (April 1955), 200–12; William L. Rowe, 'The Problem of Evil and Some Varieties of Atheism', in *The Problem of Evil*, ed. Marilyn McCord Adams and Robert Merrihew Adams (Oxford: OUP, 1990), 126–37. Brian Davies examines this area of thought in *Thomas Aquinas on God and Evil* (Oxford: OUP, 2011), 2–8.

[5] *Summa Theologiae* I, q. 2, a. 3, ad. 1.

in a memorable line, Davies likens it to asking, 'Why is humility shorter than the Eiffel Tower?'[6] It is simply the wrong question to ask. Davies continues:

> to ask whether God can be morally justified when it comes to the evils that occur is to ask a question that should never have been raised in the first place. For him, God is not to be thought of as a moral agent behaving either well or badly. [...] His point is that God is just not the sort of thing to be evaluated as we evaluate people morally, albeit that he is perfectly happy to say that God is good and just and merciful.[7]

Even if it is a flawed question, it is one that Thomas has taken seriously enough to raise and to attempt to answer, whether or not later readers care for the way he has answered it. Evil, in this regard, is, for Thomas, a small thing: something big enough to trip us up, but not something big enough to make us change course, or indeed alter in any way the route planned for us. In Thomas's rhetoric, evil is brought up, immediately to be swept away by discussion of the Five Ways; as Thomas presents it, this is a reasonable approach to take. At this point, Thomas has not yet defined evil, but we should, before we go too much further. Peter Kreeft briefly defines it like this:

> [E]vil is not a thing, an entity, a being. All beings are either the Creator or creatures created by the Creator. But everything God created is good, according to Genesis. We naturally tend to picture evil as a thing: a black cloud, or a dangerous storm, or a grimacing face, or dirt. But these pictures mislead us. If God is the Creator of all things and evil is a thing, then God is the Creator of evil, and he is to blame for its existence. No, evil is not a thing but a wrong choice, or the damage done by a wrong choice. Evil is no more a positive thing than blindness is. But it is just as real. It is not a thing, but it is not an illusion.[8]

---

[6] Davies, *Thomas Aquinas on God and Evil*, 113.

[7] idem, 114.

[8] Peter Kreeft, 'The Problem of Evil', in *Fundamentals of the Faith: Essays in Christian Apologetics* (San Francisco: Ignatius Press, 1988), 54.

Evil is real, but not a thing, but also not an illusion. It is therefore not bound to size or dimension as such, but speaking analogically, we can conceive of a 'great evil', or 'the lesser of two evils'. But what does it mean to say that evil is 'real'? Augustine, in the *Enchiridion*, as quoted above by Thomas, has evil in the world as a result of God's permissive will: it can be said that God 'allows' evil, which on the face of it seems inadequate and insufficient terminology, but that assertion cannot be separated from the context in which God does so because, and only because, God's 'omnipotence and goodness [are] such as to bring good even out of evil.'

Morwenna Ludlow and Adam Couchman examine how this is considered in the writings of the Cappadocian Fathers:[9] Gregory of Nyssa considered that evil 'has no substance of its own; apart from deliberate choice evil exists nowhere.'[10] And since it is insubstantial in this way, both Gregory of Nyssa and Basil of Caesarea agree that, as Ludlow puts it, 'evil is a characteristic of a rational being's choice to turn against God'.[11] For Couchman, this places a paradox at the heart of Gregory's thought: 'The Divine is limitless and so there is a logical impossibility of anything being outside of the Good, yet at the same time evil does have a presence, or at the very least an effect within creation.' And, while this 'demands an explanation', the answer, for Gregory, 'must not find its origin in the Divine will'.[12] Ludlow, writing on demons in Cappadocian thought, points us to an answer: a demon 'remains related to God ontologically because …

---

[9] Morwenna Ludlow, 'Demons, Evil and Liminality in Cappadocian Theology', *Journal of Early Christian Studies*, 20/2 (2012), 179–211; Adam Nicholas Couchman, '"In the image of the Image": Theological Anthropology and its Importance for Christian Holiness According to Gregory of Nyssa' (MA dissertation, University of Manchester, 2011), chapter II, 'Evil, the Fall and the Human Condition', 39ff.

[10] Gregory of Nyssa, *The Lord's Prayer, The Beatitudes*, trans. Hilda C. Graef, ed. Johannes Quasten and Joseph Plumpe, Ancient Christian Writers, 18. (New York: Paulist Press, 1954), 135–6.

[11] Morwenna Ludlow, 'Demons, Evil and Liminality', 187.

[12] Adam Couchman, "In the image of the Image", 41.

God remains eternally lord of the entire created world', but neverthe-less a demon has a will that is 'completely opposed to God'.[13]

Evil is not a thing. It has no substance. It is an adjective, not a noun. A particular adjective may be appropriate or inappropriate according to context: it may be too intense or too flat; it may sometimes be sur-prisingly appropriate precisely because the 'wrong' word is used. The Warrant from Charles II for the building of St Paul's Cathedral describes Christopher Wren's design as 'very artificial, proper, and useful'.[14] Today, as meaning and association change over time, these words sound more appropriate for a suburban garage extension. Here, I want to explore what happens if we regard evil as referring to, or character-istic of, smallness. I do not wish to argue that this is the only way to see or to depict evil; instead, I want to consider what happens when we do regard it this way, and what can make depictions of evil as small, and an understanding of evil as small, compelling.

## Mounting-blocks and stumbling-blocks

I find some support for this approach in St Matthew's Gospel. After the declaration of Peter (Matt. 16:13–20), Jesus explains to the disciples 'that he must go to Jerusalem and suffer many things from the elders and chief priests and scribes, and be killed, and on the third day be raised' (Matt. 16:21). Indeed, it is more than didactic explanation: the word used as the devil shows Jesus the kingdoms of the world (Matt. 4:8) is 'δεικνύειν [deiknuein]', a verb of showing, as the leper, now cleansed, is to show himself to the priest (Mark 1:44), as Jesus showed the disciples His hands and His side, at which they rejoiced (John 20:20). After this 'showing', 'Peter took him and began to rebuke him, saying, "God forbid, Lord! This shall never happen to you." But he turned and said to Peter, "Get behind me, Satan! You are a hindrance to me; for you are not on the side of God, but of men." (Matt. 16:22–3).

---

[13] Morwenna Ludlow, 'Demons, Evil and Liminality', 193.

[14] Stephen Wren, *Parentalia: Or, Memoirs of the Family of the Wrens* (London: Osborn, 1750), 281. This is probably the source of the apocryphal descrip-tion of the cathedral as 'amusing, awful, and artificial'.

'Hindrance' is the RSV's translation of the Greek 'σκάνδαλον [skan-dalon]'. Other translations include: 'offence' (Authorised Version); 'stone that could make me stumble' (Common English Bible); 'obstacle in my way' (Good News Bible); 'obstacle in my path' (Jerusalem Bible); 'stumbling block' (NRSV); 'scandal' (Douay-Rheims); 'a cause of stumbling' (Wycliffe). In German, Martin Luther (1545) gave 'Du bist mir ärgerlich'—'you are an annoyance to me'. The Latin Vulgate has *scandalum*. This word is perhaps best known as it is used by St Paul: 'we preach Christ crucified, a *stumbling block* to Jews and folly to Gentiles, but to those who are called, both Jews and Greeks, Christ the power of God and the wisdom of God' (1 Cor. 1:23–4).

Here, the vagaries of biblical translation come into view: both longer English quotations are from the RSV, and yet in the one we have 'hindrance', and in the other, 'stumbling-block'. The range of English translations shows that we are dealing with an obstacle, or something that might make one trip up. But the translation of *skandalon* as 'stumbling-block' gave me pause. We are familiar enough with its figurative, illustrative meaning, and with the subsequent terminology of 'scandal' that arises from it; but what actually is a stumbling-block? What is the real-life concept from which the image is drawn? My own entirely subjective impression of the term is that it has something purposeful about it. It feels like something intentionally put there, in a way that a 'hindrance' or a 'stone that could make me stumble' does not. This may be so because, before thinking too deeply about this, the image I had in mind was the product of various youthful visits to National Trust properties and the like, in which the stables (now more often than not transformed into tearooms and gift shops), have outside them stone constructions called 'mounting blocks', stepped platforms to assist in mounting or dismounting, for reasons of modesty, infirmity, inexperience, or to save strain on the horse's spine. One may be seen on Pall Mall, outside the Athanaeum, and fixed to it is a metal plaque bearing the inscription 'This horseblock was erected by desire of the Duke of Wellington 1830'. Mounting blocks are deliberate constructions, some are quite grand, though modern ones are made of moulded plastic. They take up space.

Are these impressions really characteristics of the biblical *skandalon*? Yes, and no. According to the broad consensus of sundry biblical dictionaries, a *skandalon* is part of a trap that may be set by hunters or soldiers—the trigger over which an animal or enemy trips, activating the snare. It turns out, then, that there is an argument for seeing a degree of deliberation about the placing and construction of a stumbling-block, an intention or intelligence at work behind where it is and how it is encountered that is absent from the various other English-language offerings that make a *skandalon* sound like a synonym for a naturally-growing tree root which one simply did not see among the leaves or mud, or an unevenness in paving or cobbles that has come about through movement over time, or a poor choice of stone on the builder's part, or the erosion of hoggin or mortar.

We can learn something from this word: a stumbling-block is necessarily a small thing. If it were a bigger obstacle, we would just go around it; if it were too big we would turn back and find another way, or find that the way was barred forever. If you fall over a stumbling-block, what happens? You fall down. You give into weakness, sin, temptation. And then? If we are caught in a trap, we can stay caught, stay fallen down, or we can seek help to get out. The stumbling-block that Peter here embodies for Jesus—and we should not forget that these words immediately follow the phrase 'Get behind me, Satan'—is a small thing. It can have great consequences, but it is a small thing. This almost throwaway line, it seems to me, puts evil and sin in their proper place. Sin is deadly only if we let it be. But it is also true that accepting God's help requires of us that we are sufficiently humble to accept that we need it. We must acknowledge that we have fallen, instead of pretending—through pride, embarrassment, hardness of heart—that we are just resting for a moment. We must also be courageous enough to accept that the help God offers us might require a new path, a new perspective from us if it is to be effective. We will have to be more careful; we will need to change; we will need to take up our cross once more.

When Jesus tells the disciples at this point that those who wish to follow Him should 'take up their cross', the only idea of 'the cross' they have at that moment is as a means of execution for prisoners sentenced to death by the Romans. What would a handful of Galilean fishermen even know of such things? What on earth could that have to do with the Christ, the Son of the living God? Those who say 'take up our cross' should remember just how hard a saying it was for those who heard it the first time. So the lesson given us here is not a platitude; it is a difficult but necessary lesson in humility and courage: whatever happens, however hard we fall, we can always be raised up.

## Evil: fungal and banal

Despite this, the fact remains that, if we have stumbled over a *skandalon*—however cleverly placed—it is a small thing that has caused us to fall. To see evil as small is not to denigrate its effects, to play down the suffering of those caught up in it, or to diminish the point or magnitude of salvation from it. Think of Hannah Arendt's *Eichmann in Jerusalem: A Report on the Banality of Evil*.[15] To call evil 'banal' is to focus not on its outcome but on its agents. As Arendt herself wrote:

> It is indeed my opinion now that evil is never 'radical', that it is only extreme, and that it possesses neither depth nor any demonic dimension. It can overgrow and lay waste the whole world precisely because it spreads like a fungus on the surface. It is 'thought-defying', as I said, because thought tries to reach some depth, to go to the roots, and the moment it concerns itself with evil, it is frustrated because there is nothing. That is its 'banality'. Only the good has depth that can be radical.[16]

---

[15] Hannah Arendt, *Eichmann in Jerusalem: A Report on the Banality of Evil* (New York: Viking Press, 1964), originally serialized in *The New Yorker* in 1963.

[16] Hannah Arendt, *Letter to G. Gerhard Scholem, 3 Dec 1964*. The Hannah Arendt Papers at the Library of Congress, Correspondence: Scholem, Gershom Gerhard, 1963–1964, n.d. (Series: Adolf Eichmann File, 1938–1968, n.d.) http://memory.loc.gov/cgi-bin/ampage?collId=mharendt_pub&fileName=03/030170/030170page.db&recNum=37 (accessed 11 November 2020).

I dispute that evil 'possesses' no 'demonic dimension', but that is not of particular concern here. Arendt's point is that evil has no depth, which is why it is frustrating. As Gertrude Stein wrote, 'there is no there there'.[17] If evil 'spreads like a fungus' and does so 'on the surface', then we can still be caught up by it, still be stained or infected by it, even though it may be cobweb-light. Compare also Arendt's image of 'thought' being aimed at depth, at 'go[ing] to the roots' with how the Letter to the Ephesians described the believer as 'being rooted and grounded in love, [that you] may have power to comprehend with all the saints what is the breadth and length and height and depth' (Eph. 3:17–18). Love is capable of receiving, of supporting, the strength and growth of roots. Evil is rootless. The purpose of the stumbling-block in its hunting sense is to catch prey. What could be intentionally planted and then grow to sufficient strength that it could be used as a *skandalon* that would not also require the hunter to wait for years before it was ready to use? The hunter would have to make use of something that had already grown, say, a sapling, in which case it has not come to the maturity of being properly rooted. Or the hunter would have to break off some more supple, perhaps newer or weaker bit of a plant, in which case the rootedness of the whole plant could not save the part torn off, and, more than likely, the tearing off would not ultimately have too much of an effect on the rootedness. Once broken off, or twisted, it would then have to be put just deep enough into the ground that it would have the desired effect, with enough strength to trip or ensnare the desired prey, but not so deep that the work would take too long, make too much noise, be otherwise too conspicuous. The *skandalon* must partake in the same qualities as the fungus, as the banality; there must always be some violence in the way whatever is used as the snare is turned to that use; there must always be an impermanence to it.

We can see how these qualities are congruent with evil considered as a small thing if we have in mind, say, the bullet, or the

---

[17] Gertrude Stein, *Everybody's Autobiography* (New York: Random House, 1937), 289.

virus: even though neither of these possesses intention in a moral sense, the former can be the means of pain and suffering, and the latter, as 2020 onwards has shown us, a cause of suffering of different kinds even in those who do not suffer sickness. Physical objects and natural entities can be *part* of evil in the sense in which Thomas defines it later on in the *Summa*: 'the absence of good, taken in a privative sense, is an evil; as, for instance, the privation of sight is called blindness'.[18] They bring about privation in those who are shot or those who are infected, because they give rise to disfunction and non-being. So the means of evil need not be large, or grandiose. Neither do we need to confine our imagination of evil to the Scriptures: literary imaginings of evil can rely precisely on smallness, on mundanity, to have a particularly chilling effect, and I want to consider some examples of that, and of how they can sometimes be particularly effective, and are on other occasions robbed of their effectiveness when attempts are made to, as it were, enlarge the evil they contain.

Although John Barton considers evil in this way, as 'sub-personal', it is impossible, at this point, to ignore the ways in which evil has been personalized.[19] With Aquinas, I hold that the devil and evil cannot be said to be the same: evil is not a thing or a person.[20] The problem for literary depictions of evil is, though, precisely when all evil is loaded on to one set of diabolical shoulders. This is what I term 'making evil too big'.

## Making evil too big: Milton and Montgomery

Undoubtedly the best-known literary depiction of Satan is in *Paradise Lost*. After his first speech, he is described by Beelzebub as 'Prince', as:

---

[18] *Summa Theologiae*, I–ii, q. 18, a. 1.

[19] See John Barton, above, page 2

[20] *Summa Theologiae* I-ii, q. 80. He quotes with approval Gennadius of Massilia (*d. c.* 496): 'Not all our evil thoughts are incited by the devil; sometimes they are due to a movement of the free-will.'

> Chief of many Throned Powers,
> That led th' imbattelld Seraphim to Warr
> Under thy conduct, and in dreadful deeds
> Fearless, endanger'd Heav'ns perpetual King;
> And put to proof his high Supremacy.[21]

Beelzebub is subordinate to Satan, his 'mind and rhetoric' manipulated by him 'in order to forestall opposition to his personal ambition.'[22] We take the flattery, but retain the impression of grandeur, even fallen grandeur. By Book III, he has disguised himself, and as a ...

> ... stripling Cherube he appeers,
> Not of the prime, yet such as in his face
> Youth smil'd Celestial, and to every Limb
> Sutable grace diffus'd.[23]

In Book IV he sits on the Tree of Life 'like a Cormorant', and later he is seen 'Squat like a Toad'.[24] Finally, he is a snake, 'wily', 'sly', 'dire'.[25] And at the end? Satan's words earlier on had such power that William Blake wrote 'The reason Milton wrote in fetters when he wrote of Angels & God, and at liberty when he wrote of Devils & Hell, is because he was a true Poet and of the Devil's party without knowing it'.[26] Finally, Satan is silenced: 'he would have spoke, But hiss for hiss returnd with forked tongue'.[27] Milton's Satan dim-

---

[21] John Milton, *Paradise Lost*, Book 1, lines 128–32. Text from the Second Edition (London: S. Simmons, 1674).

[22] Robert F. Willson, Jr., '*Paradise Lost* II. 310–416: Beelzebub's Satanic Solution', *CEA Critic* 37/2 (January 1975), 12–15, p. 12, n. 4.

[23] *Paradise Lost*, Book 3, lines 636–9.

[24] *Paradise Lost*, Book 4, lines 196 and 800.

[25] *Paradise Lost*, Book 9, lines 91, 613 and 643.

[26] William Blake, *The Marriage of Heaven and Hell*, ed. with a commentary by Geoffrey Keynes (Oxford: OUP, 1975), xvii.

[27] *Paradise Lost*, Book 10, lines 517–18.

inishes before our very eyes. What lies at the heart of *Paradise Lost*? Stanley Fish identifies this as the 'reading experience' which 'becomes the felt measure of man's loss', whereby '[t]hrough process of trial and error we become better able to understand our limitations and ultimately, perhaps, to transcend them'.[28] For A. D. Nuttall, we should pay attention to the 'movement into live morality' at the work's end.[29] In either case (or any of the other interpretations put forward over the years), something vitally important would be missing if Satan were to have remained at the end essentially unchanged from the beginning. For Milton, the victory of Christ is not about a battle between two individuals, equally matched, with an uncertain outcome. Jesus Christ is not another individual like any other: though he is first described as 'one greater Man',[30] the point of the Incarnation is that he is the 'heavenly Word proceeding forth, / Yet leaving not his Father's side'.[31] In a quite different context, St Cyril of Jerusalem (313–386 AD) offers a useful corrective to such individual-focussed thinking:

> Wondrous indeed it was, that one who was blind from his birth should receive sight in Siloam; but what is this compared with the blind of the whole world? A great thing it was, and passing nature, for Lazarus to rise again on the fourth day; but the grace extended to him alone, and what was it compared with the dead in sins throughout the world? Marvellous it was, that five loaves should pour forth food for the five thousand; but what is that to those who are famishing in ignorance through all the world? It was marvellous that she should have been loosed who had been bound by Satan eighteen years: yet what is this to all of us, who

---

[28] Stanley Eugene Fish, 'Not so much a teaching as an intangling': Milton's Method in *Paradise Lost*', in *Milton: Modern Judgements*, ed. Alan Rudrum (London: Macmillan, 1968), 104–35, p. 127.

[29] A. D. Nuttall, 'Everything is Over before it Begins' (review of Stanley Fish, *How Milton Works*), *London Review of Books*, 23/12 (21 June 2001).

[30] *Paradise Lost*, Book 1, line 4.

[31] St Thomas Aquinas, *Verbum Supernum*, trans. J. M. Neale. See: *New English Hymnal* no. 269.

were fast bound in the chains of our sins? But the glory of the Cross led those who were blind through ignorance into light, loosed all who were held fast by sin, and ransomed the whole world of mankind.[32]

In the end, Satan should not be the focus of our attention: why stare at an impotently hissing snake when we could fix our eyes on the Son of God?

Milton's Satan is miserable, inspiring revulsion and pity. By contrast, the Satan of Robert Montgomery's epic, *Satan, A Poem*, is risible, and not as the author intended.[33] In Book 1 he surveys the world—from Jerusalem, Baghdad, Heliopolis, to Russia as invaded by Napoleon (of whom Satan approves), to India, to 'yon Canadian woods / Whose stately poplars clothe their heads with clouds'[34] and finally to England. Book II is a consideration of nature and God. Here, Satan describes himself in relation to the Almighty: 'A doleful midnight to cerulean day / Is not more opposite, than I to Thee: / Thou art the Glorious, I the Evil One; thou reign'st above; my Kingdom is below.'[35] To underline this underworldly atmosphere, Satan later speaks of 'a hell-toned feeling such as I would nurse'.[36] In Book III, Satan's attention turns to contemporary London and England. Here, some words from Richard Hengist Horne sum up Montgomery's general approach:

> Satan goes to the play. To what part of the house is not said. His natural locality would of course be the pit [...] but as Mr Montgomery clearly explains that his hero went there on business— to collect materials for this very poem—it is to be presumed that he

---

[32] *St Cyril of Jerusalem, Catechetical Lectures*, 13.1, trans. Edwin Hamilton Gifford from *Nicene and Post-Nicene Fathers*, Second Series, vol. 7, ed. Philip Schaff and Henry Wace (Buffalo NY: Christian Literature Publishing Co., 1894), rev. and ed. for New Advent by Kevin Knight. https://www.newadvent.org/fathers/310113.htm (accessed 10 May 2021).

[33] Robert Montgomery, *Satan: A Poem* (London: Samuel Maunder, 1830).

[34] Montgomery, *Satan*, line 59.

[35] idem, line 202.

[36] idem, line 243.

was in the boxes. [...] The comparison of a theatrical scene with a scene in paradise, and made by one who had actually been in both places, would be more bold than reverent in any other writer; nor are we by any means sure that Satan or his poet could show the slightest foundation for it. But we bow to their joint authority.[37]

On its publication, as the old *Dictionary of National Biography* noted, *Satan* 'commended itself strongly to the evangelical party ... and seemed likely to surpass in popularity all the poet's previous effusions. It ran through more editions, and suddenly elicited more contemporary fame than the publication of any poet since the death of Byron.'[38] Reviewers, as opposed to general readers, were not favourably impressed. An anonymous article in the *Edinburgh Review* for 1830 is characteristic:

> The motto to the Poem of Satan is taken from the Book of Job: — 'Whence comest thou? — From going to fro in the earth and walking up and down in it.' [...] With the exception, however, of this propensity to locomotion, Satan has not one Satanic quality. Mad Tom had told us, that 'the prince of darkness is a gentleman' [*King Lear*, Act 3 Scene 4]; but we had yet to learn that he is a respectable and pious gentleman, whose principle fault is, that he is something of a twaddle, and far too liberal of his good advice.[39]

That 'good advice' is Satan's explaining the awful wretchedness (and consequently his approval) of various philosophical and social positions disliked or opposed by Montgomery, aided by copious footnotes. Why pay any attention to such a bad poem, especially when we have spent time with *Paradise Lost*? The poem was very popular, and quotes Milton twice in the accompanying apparatus, as

---

[37] Richard Hengist Horne, ed., *A New Spirit of the Age, with an Introduction by Walter Jerrold* (Oxford: OUP, 1844, reprinted 1907), 420–1.

[38] Thomas Seccombe, 'Montgomery, Robert (1807–1855)', *Dictionary of National Biography* 38 (New York: Macmillan & Co., 1894), 322.

[39] '1. The Omnipresence of the Deity, a Poem. By Robert Montgomery. 2. Satan, a Poem. By Robert Montgomery', in *The Edinburgh Review* 51 (April–July 1830), 193–210, p. 209.

well as naming him directly twice in the text. It is entirely in the first person and is so constructed as to rob Satan of any impression of evil. He is ridiculous, not engaging or horrifying. He offers us neither Fish's 'reading experience' nor Nuttall's 'live morality'. He is always the same. He does not grow—and, perhaps most importantly in relation to Milton—neither does he diminish. His evil is overblown, rather than grand, and at the same time insignificant, rather than small. I find myself irresistibly reminded of the Vl'hurg invasion fleet in *The Hitchhiker's Guide to the Galaxy*:

> For thousands more years the mighty ships tore across the empty wastes of space and finally dived screaming on to the first planet they came across—which happened to be the Earth—where due to a terrible miscalculation of scale the entire battle fleet was accidentally swallowed by a small dog.[40]

## *Making evil obvious: M. R. James and E. F. Benson*

That subtlety is generally better than the obvious is surely a commonplace, but two further examples of literary evil show how this works. In the ghost stories of Montague Rhodes James, the word 'evil' is used very sparingly. And yet it is more than strongly implied or suggested. James himself explained his approach in an article for *The Bookman* in 1929:

> Reticence may be an elderly doctrine to preach, yet from the artistic point of view, I am sure it is a sound one. Reticence conduces to effect, blatancy ruins it, and there is much blatancy in a lot of recent stories. They drag in sex too, which is a fatal mistake; sex is tiresome enough in the novels; in a ghost story, or as the backbone of a ghost story, I have no patience with it. At the same time don't let us be mild and drab. Malevolence and terror, the glare of evil faces, 'the stony grin of unearthly malice', pursuing forms in darkness, and 'long-drawn, distant screams', are all in place, and so is a modicum of blood, shed with deliberation and carefully hus-

---

[40] Douglas Adams, *The Hitchhiker's Guide to the Galaxy: A Trilogy in Five Parts* (London: Heinemann, 1995), 136.

banded; the weltering and wallowing that I too often encounter merely recall the methods of M G Lewis [author of the 1796 Gothic novel *The Monk*].[41]

The reference 'glare of evil faces' is almost more direct than anything James includes in his actual stories. And it is perhaps a result of his success in applying the 'doctrine of reticence' that those stories continue to be read and adapted for television, film, and radio (where they are arguably most effective). By contrast, the 'spook-stories' of James's contemporary Edward Frederic Benson are much less well-known today. Like his comic and satirical writing, they often feature elderly bachelors or husbands of much younger wives: Philip Hope, in *The Dance*, is a malevolent, spidery iteration of Georgie Pillson from the Mapp and Lucia series of novels. 'The Hanging of Alfred Wadham', a story of just over 5,000 words, opens with Father Denys Hanbury, a Roman Catholic priest, sitting with the narrator discussing seances.[42] Hanbury goes on to tell the story of Alfred Wadham, sentenced to death for the murder of Gerald Selfe, 'a man of loose life' who 'held a respectable position'. Blackmail features prominently in the backstory. Wadham was Selfe's manservant, and the obvious suspect in his murder, though Wadham maintains his innocence. Hanbury, acting as Catholic prison chaplain, meets Wadham, who, despite being 'eager to confess other misdeeds of his, some of which it was ugly to speak of', continues to protest that 'if he was hanged he died unjustly'. On the eve of Wadham's going to the gallows, Horace Kennion comes to Hanbury to make his confession, during which he confesses to Selfe's murder. Despite Hanbury's entreaties, Kennion refuses to go to the police, because, he says,

> not long ago you were very nasty to me. [...] You told me that no decent man would consort with me. So it struck me, quite suddenly,

---

[41] M. R. James, 'Some Remarks on Ghost Stories', *The Bookman* (December 1929), 172.

[42] E. F. Benson, 'The Hanging of Alfred Wadham', in *More Spook Stories* (London: Hutchinson, 1934).

only to-day, that it would be pleasant to see you in the most awful hole. I daresay I've got Sadic [*sic*] tastes, too, and they are being wonderfully indulged.

Because of the seal of the confessional, there is nothing Hanbury can do, despite his best efforts, to prevent Wadham's hanging. In due course, Hanbury is haunted by what he takes to be Wadham's ghost, bearing the aspect of the hanged man: 'I had let him go innocent to his death, and my punishment was just.' It turns out that it is not Wadham's ghost, but the spirit of Kennion, or perhaps the evil spirit that had possessed him. Before the narrator's eyes, the spirit appears, and is driven back by Hanbury. The tale concludes as Hanbury explains to the narrator that he has been able to tell him the story, including the contents of the confession, because Kennion had taken his own life that morning, leaving behind a full account of the entire business. Hanbury's description of the haunting is graphic, as is the narrator's own account. Benson gives much of what James called 'Malevolence and terror, the glare of evil faces, "the stony grin of unearthly malice"', but is not here an adherent of the 'doctrine of restraint', especially regarding what he communicates about evil. Throughout the course of the story there are references to 'evil imaginings', a 'sense of evil power', a 'tempest of evil'. The narrator is warned 'if you see or hear anything, despise it, for it is evil'. After the climactic appearance of the ghost, Father Denys informs the narrator that 'what wore the semblance of humanity was pure evil'. Benson's story is, in the end, sordid, rather than truly chilling. The evil is too prominent, the explanation too full. M. R. James leaves dark gaps in which the reader's response is part of the thrill of reading the stories. Benson, by contrast, turns on the lights to show us how dark it is.

## Adapting evil: Henry James and Charles Dickens

As we have seen, some of the most successful ways in which writers show evil involve presenting it as small, mean, pinched: as a *skandalon* rather than a huge edifice or unbridgeable abyss. We have seen how less successful or enduring works can fail precisely because they make evil too big. I now consider adaptations of two literary works that each magnify the evil their originals contain, comparing and contrasting the effects which this creates.

Henry James's *The Turn of the Screw* has been much adapted for stage and screen and has influenced many other works.[43] The story is told by a man reading to a group of friends from the writings of his sister's governess, now dead. She is engaged to look after two children, Flora and Miles, at a country house in Essex called Bly. The house is kept up by Mrs Grose, the housekeeper. Miles comes home from school at more or less the same time a letter arrives explaining that he has been expelled. Meanwhile, the governess begins to see a couple in the estate's grounds whom in due course she takes to be the ghosts of her predecessor Miss Jessel and Peter Quint, a former employee. Put extremely briefly, sinister things happen, Flora leaves, and Miles dies. The word 'evil' is used fairly frequently: Peter Quint's time working at Bly is called 'this evil time'; the governess describes the woman she has seen as being 'of quite as unmistakeable horror and evil' as the man. Of Miss Jessel, the governess later says, 'there was not, in all the long reach of her desire, an inch of her evil that fell short'. And Miles's last words are 'Peter Quint—you devil!'

Critical views on the novella divide into 'apparitionists' and those who come 'close to impugning the governess's sanity'[44] Edmund Wilson's Freudian reading is among the best-known analyses of the book, but there are many others.[45] In Benjamin Britten's adaptation, with librettist Myfanwy Piper, part of the task was to make decisions about the psychological or supernatural aspects of James's story. Thus, the opera audience can see and hear the ghosts,

---

[43] See Adeline R. Tintner, *Henry James's Legacy: The Afterlife of his Figure and Fiction*, (Baton Rouge LA: Louisiana State University Press, 1998), 371–82.

[44] Thomas Mabry Cranfill and Robert Lanier Clark, Jr., *An Anatomy of* The Turn of the Screw (Austin TX: University of Texas Press, 1965), 5.

[45] Edmund Wilson, 'The Ambiguities of Henry James, revised', in *The Triple Thinkers* (New York: Harcourt, Brace, and Co., 1938), 122–64.

or visitants, but in both novella and opera, Mrs Grose the housekeeper does not see them. As well as decisions like this, musical factors are also involved. Britten used a twelve-note 'Screw' theme, repeated and varied throughout.[46] Though the word 'evil' is used throughout the novella, in the opera it is sung only twice, in a short song from the governess near the beginning of Act II. If there is a 1950s patina over an 1890s original, it is one that adds to, rather than detracts from, the audience's interpretative experience. Britten and Piper have given us, at this point in their adaptation, a drop of evil that is very small, but horribly effective.

In December 2019, the BBC showed a three-part adaptation by Steven Knight of Charles Dickens's 1843 novella *A Christmas Carol*. In the trailer, we pan over a gloomy London street, as a single high piano note sounds, followed by the noise of horses' hooves and threatening strings. A grim face (Scrooge) looks through a frosted window, before a figure in chains is seen, walking through a snowbound wood towards a large bonfire. Scrooge turns from the window towards the chain-bound apparition of Jacob Marley as the hands of a clock face are seen to move. The voiceover declaims 'Tonight you will not sleep. Come and look upon the evil that you did.' A scene of the distressed Cratchit family is shown. Still on voiceover, Scrooge asks, 'Who are you?', to which the voice hitherto speaking replies 'A ghost', at which point a sinister figure with long white hair and beard, wearing a battered top hat, is seen turning to look at Scrooge on a street-corner.[47] The *Guardian* described it as 'darker and more graphic than the original work' with 'an expletive-friendly script [...] which gives itself liberal license to reinvent'.[48]

[46] John Evans, 'Benjamin Britten's *The Turn of the Screw*: The Music; I. The Sketches: Chronology and Analysis', in Patricia Howard, ed., *Benjamin Britten: The Turn of the Screw* (Cambridge: Cambridge University Press, 1985), 63–70, p. 66.

[47] https://www.youtube.com/watch?v=DeoTY3j3_5s (accessed 3 January 2021).

[48] https://www.theguardian.com/commentisfree/2019/dec/23/the-guardian-view-on-the-new-scrooge-a-charismatic-antihero-for-christmas (accessed 19 December 2020).

The description of Scrooge's career and its effects as 'evil' is the point I wish to underscore. Dickens himself is sparing in his use of such terms, and the word 'evil' is never applied by any of the spirits to Scrooge or his deeds: the closest in fact is in the reaction of the 'blind men's dogs' which 'would tug their owners into doorways and up courts' at Scrooge's approach, and then 'wag their tails as though they said, "No eye at all is better than an evil eye, dark master!"' This is one of only two places in which the word 'evil' is used at all in the original text, the other being in reference to the legend of St Dunstan and the Evil Spirit.[49] Though he is described as 'a squeezing, wrenching, grasping, scraping, clutching, covetous, old sinner', the one word in the semantic field occupied by 'evil' that is directed at Scrooge is used when his earlier words to the two men collecting for the poor ('"If they would rather die", said Scrooge, "they had better do it, and decrease the surplus population"') are quoted back to him by the Ghost of Christmas Present, and described by it as 'wicked cant'. The 2019 adaptation shows Scrooge as a fully-fledged Victorian capitalist, living—existing—joylessly on the fruits of a graphically-displayed sweated labour from which he is distant and insulated. Dickens, meanwhile, left Scrooge's occupation somewhat indistinct, though his business is in Cornhill and he is known at the Royal Exchange.

This adaptation, in my view, fails ultimately because it seeks to magnify the smallness of Scrooge's evil. It names it as 'evil', which Dickens did not. The appalling hard-heartedness of Ebenezer Scrooge need not be restricted only to slavers and prosperous industrialists. Whatever it is Scrooge actually does in his business, by his redemption at the end of the story, he is generous with his wealth, but it is a wealth of benefactions, local endowments, legacies: he became as 'good a man, as the good old city knew, or any other good old city, town, or borough, in the good old world'. It is on the scale of a 'city, town, or borough', rather than a world-changing reverse

---

[49] 'St Dunstan, as the story goes, / Once pulled the devil by the nose / With red-hot tongs, which made him roar, / That he was heard three miles or more.' (folk rhyme).

on the part of a great plutocrat. Because we do not know the original Scrooge's business, it is entirely possible and legitimate to speculate that it could be tied up with all kinds of exploitation and horror throughout the world, and the fact that Dickens does not mention this may invite us to consider the 'historical valences' to which Edward Said referred in his reading of Jane Austen's *Mansfield Park* and its connection with the Atlantic slave trade, as Sir Thomas Bertram's wealth is founded on his Antiguan plantations.[50] The BBC adaptation of Dickens has obviously taken this to a fuller extent than was seen in previous versions.

The naming of evil, the outspokenness of what Dickens left unsaid, is too blunt, too obvious. It takes the moral judgement out of the viewer's mind and plasters it on the screen, and on the numerous programmes and websites where the trailer would appear before broadcast. In that sense, it does not prompt the viewer to ask, 'in what ways am I like Scrooge?', which the novella does; it says, 'Scrooge is evil', and most people are confident that they are not evil, and there the comparison is closed off. The following exchange, between Scrooge and his former fiancée, Belle, makes Dickens's point clear:

> 'Another idol has displaced me; and if it can cheer and comfort you in time to come, as I would have tried to do, I have no just cause to grieve.' 'What Idol has displaced you?' he rejoined. 'A golden one.' 'This is the even-handed dealing of the world!' he said. 'There is nothing on which it is so hard as poverty; and there is nothing it professes to condemn with such severity as the pursuit of wealth!' 'You fear the world too much', she answered, gently. 'All your other hopes have merged into the hope of being beyond the chance of its sordid reproach. I have seen your nobler aspirations fall off one by one, until the master-passion, Gain, engrosses you.'

Scrooge's tragedy is that there is no room in his heart for anything other than avarice, and if we read *A Christmas Carol* as a kind

---

[50] Edward W. Said, 'Jane Austen and Empire', in *Culture and Imperialism* (London: Vintage, 1993), 107.

of parable, we see that any of us might fall prey to such a tendency—whatever the besetting vice might be that takes us over. There are stories to be told, fictional, non-fictional, and somewhere in between, about the ways in which the exploitation of others is the source of the comfortable scenes in which important works in the literary canon (or the stories of historical figures who are the subjects of biographical films or books) are set, but to make this part of an adaptation of *A Christmas Carol* misses, I think, what this little work has to say about the human condition.

## Stumbling-blocks and the Little Way

I have looked at various ways in which descriptions of evil count it as a small thing, and at ways in which the effectiveness of that smallness can be heightened or undermined. Writing about *The Turn of the Screw*, but applicable to imaginative and other responses to evil, Stephen King remarks that it contains 'secrets best left untold and things best left unsaid'.[51] It is the hinting at the secrets and the near-saying of the things unsaid that allows the audience to fill in the gaps from the recesses of their own imaginations. This, I believe, legitimizes the comparison between these literary scraps and a theological reflection on evil as a small thing. The fictional works here are largely short (with the exception of the epic poems). Dickens, Henry James and E. F. Benson produced much longer works about quite different subjects; M. R. James was primarily a scholar; Montgomery was better known in his lifetime for his earlier works and for his fashionable clerical career (and is today remembered hardly at all). Only of Milton can it be said that his depiction of evil is truly lasting, and it is the one that concludes by reducing that evil to a mute and crawling thing. Yet we can see how each of these works can be likened to a *skandalon*: a tripping-hazard, something to make us stumble. They may contain significant moral lessons, or allude to great wickedness, or remind us how both these things can take place in the smallest of spheres—the domestic, the

---

[51] Stephen King, *Danse Macabre* (Berkeley CA: Berkeley Books, 1983), 50.

personal, the human heart. And yet we can pass over them as easily as, at the beginning of the *Summa*, Aquinas passes over evil in order to spend more time on God. It could well be argued that such an approach would be spiritually, morally, naïve. To recognize the existence of the stumbling-block is necessary. But to treat the stumbling-block, not as an impassable barrier of immense importance, and instead to concentrate on getting up after the fall, rather than on either the fall itself or the fear of falling, is exactly the spiritual counsel of St Thérèse of Lisieux:

> If God wants you to be as weak and powerless as a child, do you think your merit will be any less for that? Resign yourself, then, to stumbling at every step, to falling even, and to being weak in carrying your cross. Love your powerlessness, and your soul will benefit more from it than if, aided by grace, you were to behave with enthusiastic heroism and fill your soul with self-satisfaction.[52]

The best modern example of the *skandalon*, in terms of spiritual and moral development, is the German *Stolperstein* project, begun in 1992.[53] *Stolperstein* means 'stumbling stone' or 'stumbling block'. These are ten-centimetre cubes of concrete, each bearing a brass plate on which is engraved the name and dates of victims of National Socialism. Placed most commonly in front of the buildings in which the individuals or families lived or worked before deportation, execution or escape, the *Stolpersteine* literally stand out from the ground, and are also distinguished by the colour of brass. By 2019, over 75,000 had been laid in over 2000 sites throughout Europe. Joseph Pearson writes that 'the inscription is insufficient to conjure a person. It is the emptiness, void, lack of information, the maw of the forgotten, which gives the monuments their power and lifts them from the banality of a statistic.'[54]

---

[52] See Christopher O'Mahony, ed., *St Thérèse of Lisieux by Those Who Knew Her* (Dublin: Veritas, 1975), 250.

[53] See: http://www.stolpersteine.eu/en (accessed 4 May 2021).

[54] Joseph Pearson, 'Nazi Victims and Stumbling Blocks to Memory', *The Needle* (23 August 2010), https://needleberlin.com/2010/08/23/nazi-victims-and-stumbling-blocks-to-memory (accessed 14 May 2021).

These stumbling-blocks are not there to be ignored, but neither are they there to stop us in our tracks. If we fall over them perhaps (as I can attest), as visitors to, or inhabitants of places we thought we knew well, finding a newly-placed *Stolperstein* in front of a building we frequent, we have to get up again. It is important to say that such an experience would be different for a victim—and for a perpetrator—than one at an historical distance. The fact that evil *can* be a *skandalon*, *can* be a small thing, does not mean it always is, and it does not mean either that the repentance, forgiveness, or recovery of one who has caused evil, pain, suffering, should be dismissed as also a small thing. It does not trivialize the act or its effects. Evil remains, in Flannery O'Connor's words, 'a mystery to be endured'. For their intended purpose, the *Stolpersteine* do not need to be any bigger than they are. They are objects of immense power, precisely because they compel us to think about what happens next. This is a way in which evil can be small, and this is how we can come to see that getting up, by the grace of God, is what matters.

*Stolperstein for Edith Klein (St Teresa Benedicta of the Cross OCD)*

# SPEAK NO EVIL

## James Ramsay

THIS IS A REFLECTION on some of the ways in which as individuals and collectively we speak, or fail to speak, about evil, and how this relates to our ability to discern and address evil. Part of the difficulty of writing on this subject is that it might be taken to imply the writer considers him- or herself free of the sins they identify, and others. I hope what I say will not be taken to imply any such thing.

I do not directly discuss supernatural possession, exorcism and the like, as our language in respect of these is familiar from Biblical, liturgical, and wider literature. How we interpret that language is of course complex, and different cultures bring different traditional understandings to it. As a parish priest in East London, I was aware for instance of how seriously witchcraft and curses matter in some communities. Meanwhile society as a whole, in promoting a positive image of itself, can display an atavistic sense that if we refrain from speaking about social evils they do not exist. Conversely the sensationalizing of individual evils might be said to constitute a 'work of the devil' in the way it distorts and deflects attention from evils that, though in many ways greater, are more socially normalized.

I likewise do not look at 'satanism', which commonly manifests as a negative image of certain mainstream religious practices; or 'new paganism', which just as revealingly seems to bring out in some Christians a deep and aggressive insecurity about their faith. Nor do I examine the traditionally invoked personal evils of 'sex and violence', 'the demon drink', 'drugs' et al., though these are indeed hellish for individuals and their loved ones, and require steadfast prayer and disciplined therapeutic commitment to overcome.

My focus here is rather the character of systemic evil within working democracies, where every individual shares responsibility for the health of the overall polity. I reflect on how we address and fail to address evil that is under our noses yet somehow too big or unfocussed as 'problems' to be easily grasped. This is both a practical issue and a mystery, an aspect of what the German philosopher and scholar of religion Rudolf Otto called *Mysterium tremendum*,[1] the fundamental matrix of our sense of the holy—or what in more Pauline language we might describe as the spiritual economy of 'flesh', the *soma psychikon*.

## Language as more than verbal communication

As a child I was fascinated and slightly repelled by a little wood carving in my grandmother's sitting room, of three monkeys, one with its paws over its eyes, one with its paws over its ears, the third with the paws over its mouth. 'See no evil, hear no evil, speak no evil', my grandmother would wink. Later, when an older cousin asked me over the drinks tray, 'What's your sin?', I came back at him in my wobbly adolescent voice, 'Whisky. No water or ice.' Sin was cool.

But the mischievous trio continued to tease. I felt the monkey not seeing me was listening, the deaf one watching, the mute one thinking all kinds of malice. At the same time I thought it was a thoroughly good thing to have no truck with evil. I was confused.

---

[1] Cf. *Das Heilige: Über das Irrationale in der Idee des Göttlichen und sein Verhältnis zum Rationalen* (Munich: C. H. Beck, 1917), trans. John W. Harvey as *The Idea of the Holy: An Inquiry into the Non-Rational Factor in the Idea of the Divine and its Relation to the Rational* (Oxford: OUP, 1923), 12.

I was further confused by wider associations—my grand-mother's tales of life in Paris and then Rome in the 1930s, where my grandfather, who died when I was seven, was the Reuters correspondent. What had he seen, heard, and said—and not said—in Fascist Italy? My grandmother's stories of Mussolini's rallies gripped me, and I felt a thrill of horror at how, as the situation edged toward war, the friendly local shopkeepers no longer spoke to her. She and my mother, aged sixteen, eventually left for France with whatever they could carry in suitcases. Captivated by images of their overcrowded refugee boat from Marseille being bombed until nearly into British waters, I had no abstract concept of evil.

The monkeys presumably did not date from the Rome years, there would surely have been higher priorities for the suitcases. Yet words, ideas, and feelings create unconscious connections. I came to equate authoritarianism with their cheap ugliness. My grandmother's account of her feelings when trapped in a crowd at a Fascist rally affects my feelings about crowds to this day. My assumptions about journalistic integrity (my grandfather went from Rome to neutral Lisbon) clashed with later questioning of the nature and possibility of objectivity. Annoyed at myself for trying to prove to my cousin I was no stupid teenage simian, I worked harder to appear sophisticated. Unaware how sheltered my life was, I dismissed evil as monkey business.

Evil cannot be solved like a mathematical problem: our concept of evil, as opposed to a computer glitch, a flaw in logic, or juridical illegality, is grounded in experience and engagement with life. A moral code, such as the Ten Commandments, in itself only forestalls the consequences of evil rather than addressing evil *per se*. And codes tend to precipitate their own evils, giving rise to a culture of legalistic hair-splitting that Lucifer, the Angel of Light, uses most effectively to distract from the essential task of righteousness.

Moral codes in one form or another are nevertheless as essential to goodness as our skeleton is to our organs. Jesus came not to abolish the law, but to 'fulfil' it: the grace that makes a legal code an instrument of the good rather than a mechanism for tyranny is a mystery organically indwelling matter through order, pattern, proportion, balance. In Trinitarian theology this grace is not externally imposed, it flows ('begotten' ... 'proceeding' ... ) from the heart of Being. And the Trinitarian formula itself, though indeed authoritative for the majority of Christians, is not just a cerebral definition, but a negotiated creedal 'symbol' (using the technical term) of agreement about how we can speak of an ultimate inexpressible mystery. It begins, 'We believe', not 'we know' or 'assert', and concludes with 'Amen'. In short there is a mysterious continuity between the mundane world of laws, codes and constitutions, and a Kingdom 'not of this world'.

## The spiritual and the ethical

At Christmas 'mercy and truth are met together, righteousness and peace have kissed each other' (Ps. 85). Yet how is this at-onement incarnated in our lives? We need both a language for the spiritual (truth/peace) and a language for the ethical (mercy/righteousness). A discourse of truth without mercy leads to merciless ideology. The converse, all mercy with no truth, leads to a culture of indiscriminate indulgence. Similarly, righteousness must be complemented by peace if justice is to be more than mere assertion of power, while peace with no concern for righteousness is a pseudo-peace achieved by not holding evil-doers to account.

In today's pluralist world, however, there is no common spiritual language, and the ethical language of human rights and international law is far from universally accepted. For many people spiritual language is vitiated by past abuses of religion in all faiths; atheist utopianism is similarly tarred; and ethical and constitutional language ultimately rests on *a priori* assumptions that reflect unquantifiable spiritual, or at least non-purely-rational, beliefs—in the American Declaration of Independence, for instance, 'the Laws of Nature and of Nature's God' and 'We hold these Truths to be *self-evident*, that all Men are *created* equal ...' [my italics]. The Preamble to the Universal Declaration of Human Rights likewise asserts 'inherent dignity', 'the equal and inalienable rights of all members of the human family', and 'the conscience of mankind', language increasingly contested even in liberal democratic societies.

## *Spiritual vocabulary and the dynamic of language*

By the very state of public discourse therefore pronouncements about ultimate ethical and spiritual value are problematic. Yet there are different forms of 'language'. In marketing, which manipulates basic instincts through aesthetic and technological inventiveness, verbal communication is simply one ingredient. 'Evil', for instance, is a powerful weapon in the arsenal of propaganda: George W. Bush's 'axis of evil' appealed to gut emotions and prejudices, it was a tribal identifier, pointing to a 'them' who threaten 'us'. Genocide in its absolute nature may be uncontroversially denounced as evil. Yet where does evil begin? As Turkey/Armenia, and today the plight of the Uighurs and Rohingya demonstrate, 'genocide' is politically disputed.

Child abuse is undoubtedly evil. Yet tabloid-style condemnation promotes 'our' identity as decent members of a virtuous society, deflecting us from considering how far 'we' (in the UK for the sake of discussion) are ourselves perpetrating evil. Despite historically exceptional national prosperity, we accept levels of poverty that result in thousands of children being malnourished. Statistically these children will be more susceptible to major health problems in adulthood and have ten to fifteen years shorter life expectancy than those brought up with more material advantages. At what point does malnourishment become starvation, or 'fiscal prudence' that shortens lives become evil? Are the purportedly greater evils of 'financial recklessness' and 'dependency on government handouts' honest arguments?

Over the centuries spiritual language has sparked hatred, discrimination, and bloodshed, and in some societies still does. Thus 'evil' tends not to be deployed in mainstream public debate except in the most empty idiomatic sense. Right and wrong, should and should not, must and must not, are happily bandied, but spiritual language is too contentious. 'Evil' skids into hate speech. Public discourse remains within objective legally-accountable boundaries, with spiritual and religious beliefs a private matter of personal motivation. But this neat distinction hardly stands up to scrutiny.

## *The language beneath the rhetoric*

In Western culture the basis for understanding the world and for spiritual and ethical argument was for centuries the authority of inspired 'individuals', Moses, Aristotle, Galen, Ptolemy et al.; very different from our modern reliance on observation through personal experience, philosophical freedom, and medical, psychological, and sociological research all applied in a spirit of reason. This shift fundamentally changed how things were judged to be good or evil.

Reason, however, has not dispelled unconscious fears and prejudices. Though congenital disabling conditions are no longer considered evidence of hidden sin, stigma remains virulent. Where once individuals and whole social classes were deemed superior or inferior by virtue of bloodstock, social conditioning has been demonstrated to be crucial in determining human development: yet rich countries' arms industries, proxy wars, and continuing extraction of resources from poor countries suggest that despite more respectful diplomatic vocabulary, 'other' races are still viewed as they were when black-skinned people—even though it was conceded they possessed souls—were less than fully 'human'.

Meanwhile ancient forms of philosophical determinism have received new currency by developments in genetics and neuroscience, promoting the view that free will is illusory[2]. Alongside this challenge to the very principle of moral agency, that at its most extreme cuts away the ground upon which any action can be called good or bad, traditional notions of the world and what it is to be human are also being profoundly reconfigured. Whether in the unsettling exhilaration of quantum uncertainty, the ethical dilemmas of stem cell research, or the excitements and dangers of a discourse around artificial intelligence that reduces emotions and intuitions to essentially quantitative processes, the view of human beings as creatures of spiritual grace and destiny is sidelined. Those who hang on to faith, it is argued, are simply afraid to face reality.

---

[2] See, for example, *Free Will* (New York: Free Press, 2012) by the neuroscientist and author Sam Harris.

Post-Enlightenment values with their claims to universal ethical criteria are similarly beleaguered, questioned alike by authoritarian political regimes, academic decolonial studies, relativist thinkers, and biological determinists. Liberal democracies are criticized for covert economic imperialism—and it has to be said, the difficulties poor countries experience in making their voice heard substantiate the critique: when issues are recognized at the G7 summit or the World Economic Forum meaningful response is rare and then difficult to implement.

Liberal democratic discourse has a welcome emphasis on respect for differences. Yet this throws up further evils as passions become enflamed over linguistic hygiene. At the same time the reaction against 'political correctness', often in the name of freedom of expression, has coincided with a revival of intellectual resort to unquestioned authority—whether of canonical texts such as the Bible and the Qur`an, literalistically read, or partisan ideas and cultural concepts such as the 'new atheism' or ethno-religious identity. Much of the attraction of populist authoritarians like Vladimir Putin and Donald Trump seems to lie in their obvious contempt for liberal language. The traditional liberal virtues of reasoned debate, negotiation, and concern for minority perspectives have in recent years proved relatively powerless against political and financial interests that have led to a more polarized society and more illiberal politics.

The discourse of 'fake news' and 'conspiracy theories' has grown as the traditional media has declined in importance. A hallowed tenet of the liberal democratic ethos used to go thus: 'I may detest what you say, but I shall defend to the death your right to say it'. Recent stand-offs between governments and social media providers are putting this to the test. Lying and hateful speech, unaccountable to any overarching legal or moral authority, now has an instant global audience in a way that was impossible pre-internet. Once online, mischievous rumour and financially or politically-motivated 'disinformation' have massive political clout. In the end is some form of censorship the only way to protect freedom of speech? It is

surely crunch point when 'freedom of expression' is invoked to protect voices that are effectively calling for the destruction of the kind
of society in which all views can be freely expressed. Yet who has the
moral authority to police the internet for 'the good of the people'? And
to whom would those 'police' be accountable? Meanwhile, largely invisible, are those for whom the language that really 'speaks' is money.
Increasingly subtle and intrusive digital data manipulation, aimed at
generating profits, and potentially also greater political control, are
matched only by the willingness of internet users to surrender their
privacy for the benefits of greater convenience and consumer 'value'.

For those of us, whatever our vocation, whose concern is for the
spiritual wellbeing and wholeness of the world that 'God so loved',
there are perhaps two major temptations to be resisted here: on the
one hand by going on the spiritual warpath and trying to evangelize
the world out of its problems, we risk simply adding to the Babel. On
the other hand by pulling up the drawbridge of our 'interior castle'[3]
we risk misconstruing a spirituality that is anything but a retreat from
reality: lacking the structure and rigour of a life commitment to con-
templative prayer, most of us are at risk of foundering in the deep
emotional force of our own religious 'answer' to the world. Rather
we need to pay Caesar what is Caesar's, that is, contribute faithfully
what we can to the secular discourse of the world, never shying from
the objective vulnerability and constant testing of compassion that
are integral to Christian love. We need to render unto God what is
God's: affirming in our own living and speaking the reality of a love
not of this world.

## Social divisions aggravated by loss of linguistic cohesion

It is surely right that civil discourse should occlude language ineradi-
cably associated with oppression and violence. Yet this check upon
articulation of deep feelings and beliefs in mainstream public discourse

---

[3] Cf. *The Interior Castle, the Great Sixteenth-century Meditation on the Mystical
Life by St Teresa of Avila, translated by the Benedictines of Stanbrook* (New York:
Cosimo Classics, 2007).

has driven some of those feelings and beliefs underground, contributing to the proliferation of conspiracy theories and hostility to a 'deep state' of corrupt 'élites'. Cleansing the spiritual from the institutions of politics and public administration has arguably helped push opposed communities of outlook into marginalized sectional bunkers with no forum for meeting, mixing, and learning from each other. The internet is a marvellous potential means of interconnection, yet it also reinforces divisions, with self-selecting virtual communities of like-minded people being experienced as in a sense more 'real' than actual physical community. Unlike live debate, in which the human face of the opposition is always a reality and in which norms of civil discourse have to be upheld to avoid descent into physical violence, online debate lacks a human face: insults cause no obvious pain, the opposition is simply words on the screen, people are not people but game-character avatars. The internet also makes it easier to avoid debate entirely, as we spend time seeking out and 'liking' content that amuses us or confirms and nourishes our prejudices, rather than fact-checking stories that chime with our views and hunting out and evaluating opposing arguments or other perspectives.

In a culture that views the non-rational as having no place in the practical running of society, the supra-rational is not differentiated from the irrational. Ecumenical and interfaith dialogue, in which profound differences are debated patiently, knowledgeably, and respectfully, are treated as effectively on a par with irrational opinion (it might be noted that mainstream religious bodies also largely tend to ignore that dialogue). Religious extremism is seen by those in power as a secular, social and political problem, with seemingly minimal regard for theological understandings that might help at least in combating 'radicalisation'. And 'alternative' spiritualities, which in different forms—such as reverence for creation—have wide appeal and ever clearer relevance to environmental and climate issues, are routinely disparaged in the world of power politics, as in thatof much institutional religion. The world of beliefs and values, whether positive or negative, is 'balkanized' and cut off from the world of power and influence. The spiritual and the ethical cease to nourish each other, to the detriment of both. Among those with religious beliefs, many feel forced into effectively denying the inherently societal element of faith or entrenching into a religious or spiritual identity dangerously detached from wider thinking and relationships.

With 'evil' little more than a word of demonization, implicitly affirming the sense of superiority and hatred felt by those who use it, people concerned for measured argument use it with caution. Seemingly neutral language can itself, however, conceal irrational feelings that should properly be subject to a discipline of spiritual restraint. The urban riots that took place across England in August 2011 were immediately denounced by Prime Minister David Cameron as straight criminality. Yet within days the government was admitting it was not so simple. Destructive criminality there certainly was. But 'criminality' was not merely a statement of fact, it was intended to rally outrage. It entirely ignored the impact of government austerity cuts on low-income communities. Soon afterwards large amounts of public money were quietly directed into measures to compensate, to some extent, for services that had been withdrawn or drastically reduced in those areas. The evil of looting and vandalism had brought an establishment response that in its complacency and deafness to 'the cry of the poor', to use Old Testament prophetic phraseology, represented another form of evil.

The government's austerity policies had been criticized on many counts, from being economically misguided to being 'uncaring'—a word bordering on the spiritual. But there is no effective platform for spiritual critique of 'the system', in terms of the nexus of sins that produces a kneejerk response of self-exculpatory condemnation when a 'strong' comment is required on urban riots. Archbishops might be quoted, but any call by them for repentance at the top as well as the bottom of society would draw gleeful vitriol about 'those who live in glass houses'. Especially in the wake of so many egregious sexual abuse revelations, not to mention standard flak about the wealth of Church institutions, the moral credibility of establishment Churches at the level of media discourse is almost zero.

Taking the traditional Seven Deadly as a guide, it might be said the rioters had demonstrated the sins of greed, pride (lawlessness), envy, anger …, and officialdom those of pride, vanity, sloth (lack of response to warnings about collective frustration and outrage at police attitudes), wrath, and perhaps greed (the never-to-be-forgotten political imperative to attract voters). But sin-words tend not to be applied to white-collar workers unless things have gone spectacularly wrong—bankers were fair game for 'greed' for a while in 2008, but once the banks had been bailed out and the country had not collapsed, time was called (by bankers!) on the sin language, and all reverted well nigh to life as before. Except for the ever-spreading loss of public goods. 'Lessons will be learned.' Sadly, as with religious confession, lessons articulated are not necessarily learned.

## Evil's need for excitement

The dramatic and melodramatic attract attention. By contrast it is supremely difficult to talk about goodness and evil in ways that do not sensationalize and trivialize. In one of her notebooks Simone Weil observes: 'Imaginary evil is romantic and varied; real evil is gloomy, monotonous, barren, boring. Imaginary good is boring; real good is always new, marvellous, intoxicating.'[4] Most of us are probably at times tempted by the 'romantic and varied'. Hot, weird, outrageous, shocking … the headlines play to our susceptibility to enticement, our fondness for judging others, our unacknowledged pleasure in sensual titillation, our delight in being able to feel there is someone out there more 'not normal' than the self within us of which we are ashamed. Only slightly less potent is the temptation to see all that feels 'new, marvellous, intoxicating' as good (I shall return later to this inversion of Simone Weil's important point). Nothing exemplifies the attraction of drama for its own sake better than the dismissive phrase 'yesterday's news'. Scandal, coup, or murder, if the media we 'consume' reported on it yesterday, it has passed through our system and we crave more.

---

4 Simone Weil, *Gravity and Grace*, trans. Emma Crawford and Mario von der Ruhr (London: Routledge, 1952, reprinted 2002), 70.

The trashy fascination of relatively trivial evil often eclipses greater evils, both in media coverage and the court of judgement within our own minds. A minor incident can trigger a massacre or war, but the force of the irruption will almost certainly have come from a history of unaddressed grievances and pressures. Traditional spiritual teaching urges watchfulness against evil, but this needs translating into concrete terms. A work consultant helped me greatly once with the observation that we can become so caught up with what is urgent that we neglect what is important. This in turn precipitates the next generation of urgent.

I illustrate from my own experience as a parish priest how instability is thus perpetuated. The housing estate of Blackbird Leys on the edge of Oxford became notorious in 1991 when riot police were sent in to stop night-time joyriding. People had long expressed concern about social inequalities and problems in the area, but acceptable language, however insistently delivered, had had little impact. The estate was the size of a small town in itself, but had been designed with only two roads linking it to the wider city. People talked about being 'on' or 'off' the estate as if it were an island. And when I had arrived in the parish there were no road signs anywhere pointing to Blackbird Leys. For a week or so the two access roads had police checkpoints, and in the early hours of the morning more police came in to suppress displays of illegal driving deliberately put on to goad them. The drama attracted international media coverage. The 'dark underbelly' of a place world-famous for learning and privilege ... irresistible!

'Riots' was an entirely journalistic description. The all-age crowds watching the 'displays' were an audience, naughty but in no way rioting. Nevertheless on the back of 'riots' money flowed into the estate from government, business, National Lottery ... as long as we spoke the lingo of 'deprivation' and 'problems', tropes that inevitably further embedded stigma. Criminal, anti-social, dangerous actions by a few young people enabled significant amounts of money to be invested in the community for at least the next five years. Then it tailed off, and people joked, 'We need more riots.' Were those young people evil?

## Exclusion inviting the language of violence

Many had little hesitation in expressing condemnation. But what lessons had been learned? Criminality works, and problems can be paid off? At a less parochial level, the same dilemma about criminality and evil is exemplified by the suffragette/suffragist divide. Or more controversially, Malcolm X vis-à-vis Martin Luther King in the American Civil Rights movement. Or Latin American Liberation theologians' rejection of obedient ministry within the status quo. Violence as a form of 'language' against injustice must be seen in the context of societies in which the discourse of politicians, police and military, and the judiciary, has ceased to function for the common good, and respect for that discourse has been forfeited by corruption, exclusion, and (ultimately always violent) suppression—and in which Churches are widely seen as either reinforcing evil or, at best, as 'the opium of the masses', offering other-worldly consolation in 'a heartless world'.

The difficulty of attempting to remedy evil from within 'the system' was ironically further exemplified for us in Blackbird Leys through the laudable requirement for local residents to be fully involved in discussions about community improvements. Despite focus groups, consultations, and imaginative community research events, in the end involvement entailed speaking a language of outcomes, outputs, social capital, and community capacity building almost as arcane as *homoousios* vs *homoiousios*—a language creating its own professional bubbles and exclusion.

Language is power, and part of its power for evil is when its communicative function is subverted as in marketing and political manipulation. Probably the most powerful universal 'language', however, is simple animal fear. From fear of imprisonment, torture, and murder to fear of being sued, of loss of status or comfort and security, of social ostracism or merely appearing ridiculous, we put our paws over our mouths when it comes to speaking out against evil. Journalists around the world risk everything to 'speak truth to power', and as the fate of brave individuals such as Kamal Khashoggi and Daphne Caruana Galizia reminds us, some pay with their lives.

Religious voices have been similarly silenced—though as has been indicated already, the moral voice of official religious bodies is also undermined by other factors. Shamefully, where the Church has had power in society it has a long history of abusing that power and suppressing critics. Finally media ownership is a hardly insignificant matter. In capitalist democracies the media's role in holding the powerful to account is undermined not by state censorship but by 'bread and circuses'—a meagre supply of rather less than wholemeal news, within a circus of celebrity scandals, cute animal stories, and adverts and covert commercial puffs that bring in revenue. Perhaps even more politically and morally equivocal is what the media fail to cover. I am puzzled for instance why we in the West hear so little about the murders of moderate imams around the world.

By and large Western Christians are too comfortably implicated—I speak for myself at any rate—in the structural injustices of the global economic order to speak convincingly against systemic evils. Dom Helder Camara remarked, 'When I feed the poor I am called a saint; when I ask why the poor are poor I am called a Communist.' While we venerate the historic saints and martyrs, most of us prefer not to ask radical questions about the present and risk drawing upon ourselves the retaliation, even if only sneers of 'virtue-signalling', of the society in which we strive to 'do our bit'.

## The invisibility cloak

Evil is perhaps less visible in the UK now than when indigence and power inequalities were more physically manifest in everyday life. Although we see evidence of evil on television and the internet, many issues are now so global and complex and often so remote from us personally, involving economic, legal, and political arguments, that many of us do not feel competent to comment on, that we hold back from saying anything. Or we vent, not checking facts or weighing our words.

Are we, however, by some collective process with which we unconsciously collude, being gulled into this sense of non-competence? Hoi polloi, stand back! Perhaps we too meekly accept accusations that we are failing to see 'the bigger picture', and assertions that 're-grettable' evils in the world must be overlooked for the benefit of our national interests—prominent examples might be arms sales and trade deals with countries on our own government's list of countries that abuse human rights, such as Saudi Arabia, Bahrain, and China. Clerics who speak out on such matters are attacked. Yet very basic human issues are often at stake, and religion and politics obviously overlap. Just as sixteenth-century reformers demanded a language 'understanded of the people', we should keep asking simple ques-tions—such as the Queen's at the LSE about the 2008 financial crisis, when she asked why, if market instabilities were so huge, nobody had noticed them. Unfortunately questions are not always answered, especially when not asked from the top. Even the Queen had to wait seven months for a response: in June 2009 Professors Tim Besley and Peter Hennessy of the British Academy, representing leading econ-omists, academics, and financial experts told the Queen (referring to the financial world in 2007/8), 'it is difficult to recall a greater example of wishful thinking combined with hubris'.[5]

Talking about evil can feel like spitting into the wind. Cushioned as most of us are in the developed world by comfort and distance from the worst consequences of political and economic evils, many of us are as if spiritually anaesthetized against their reality. We rightly think of evil in terms of personal faults and wrongdoing, but fail to think so clearly about our complicity in structural evil. This privatization of our sense of sin, often encouraged by dismal spiritual education, can lead to unwarranted and harmful guilt feelings about mere personal

---

[5] https://wwwf.imperial.ac.uk/~bin06/M3A22/queen-lse.pdf (accessed 14 May 2021). Another group, convened by Professor Geoffrey Hodgson added: 'In recent years economics has turned virtually into a branch of ap-plied mathematics ... detached from real-world institutions and events.' It identified a lack of 'Professional wisdom informed by a rich knowledge of psychology, institutional structures and historical precedents. ... Non-quantified warnings about the potential instability of the global financial system should have been given much more attention.' https://www.geoffreymhodgson.uk/letter-to-the-queen (accessed 14 May 2021).

physicality, instinctive desires, and socially embarrassing behaviour. Carefully seeking to discern what is actually evil in our actions is difficult. It is easier simply to lean toward moral indifference or masochistic self-accusation. Meanwhile the collective evils in which we all participate, like it or not, by virtue of the community dimension of human being are rarely seen in a spiritual perspective. The need for us to accept individually our share of collective responsibility applies all the more in a functioning democracy. In Western culture generally spirituality is approached broadly in terms of the person as individual. Our person as citizen is rarely taken seriously at the spiritual rather than ethical level. The personal security and comfort most of us enjoy in the UK enable us to take this interiorized spirituality for granted. Yet they derive to a considerable extent from wider societal and global issues that we consider, if we are aware of them at all, remote and not directly relevant to us personally.

The spiritual connection we have with our neighbour the other side of the world, however, is mediated by physical goods—coffee, chocolate, cotton, semiconductors—that we ingest, have next to our skin, increasingly depend upon in everyday life. Although in Christ we profess 'God with us' in physical human presence, essential commodities that link us at the basic level of our material existence, through production and consumption, are somehow not considered as having spiritual significance beyond the important but secondary ethical concerns that of course many good people do have. Our collective ethical vision is not suffused with the spiritual clarity of personal love. Other than in intercessory prayer, our neighbour remains a statistic, invisible.

If we see someone collapse in the street, most of us want to help if we can. If that 'someone' is indoors, however, we do not see them and so are not pricked by any feeling of compassion or duty. Our media by and large focusses parochially on 'the person who has collapsed in our street'. The wider world remains to a shameful degree out of sight. Terrible events are of course reported (especially from parts of the world already on our radar, for example through financial interests or former colonial connections; French news for instance often has a quite different geographical emphasis from British news). Photographs and stories of major emergencies may move us to donate to a charity, and if we care to know, the internet provides access to huge amounts of information from all over the world. But one hears of 'compassion fatigue', or the view that we have been generous enough, too generous, and it is time 'they' sorted themselves out. Thankfully many people do take a deeper interest, maybe alter personal habits. And intercessory prayer is powerful, though most of us are probably not as prayerful as we wish we were.

Seeing a person collapse on your own street, however, has a different emotional impact even when there is nothing we can do practically to help. Many people are naturally kind, but it does not always come naturally to ask why those anonymous millions, our neighbours in Christ, far away are in such distress ('Why are the poor poor?'). Sadly that is how the world 'is'. To respond in a deeper way requires active discipleship, curiosity, listening, analysis, learning boring facts, and being ready to accept that some human beings here and now really are behaving in ways we would prefer to think had been consigned to the barbaric past. The emotion commonly described as 'compassion' (feel-good selfishness, the cynical would say) is left almost entirely unstimulated by such discipleship.

Alternatively we are left with a feeling of individual powerlessness and anger against a global 'system' that appears beyond our ability to influence. Many of the terrible crises in the world are an end symptom of large-scale hidden corruption, an evil that fuels many others. However, it is extraordinarily difficult to speak about this to any purpose. Even as we become aware of it as a global problem, it is distanced from immediate affective consciousness by the complexity of the legal, economic, and political mechanisms through which it operates. Indirect beneficiaries of this complexity, often experts in the legal, financial, and consultancy professions, assure us that they are uniquely qualified to understand the issues, and that do-gooders are fatally naive. So we back away, repudiating our own instincts of revulsion at the consequences on the ground of urbanely presented political, trade, and financial arrangements that we do not have the time or expertise to analyse in detail. When we are then asked to believe that UK laws and certain UK citizens, sometimes with titles and letters after their names, actively facilitate some of those evils, if only by inaction and turning a blind eye (though often worse), we may start to feel positively resistant: surely we are an enlightened society, Lord so-and-so does so much good ... Finally, like padded clothing, self-protective 'realism' adds a yet further layer of often unconscious mental distance when we realize that genuinely standing by our principles might impact on our personal standard of living or our global punching-power as a nation.

Numerous reports have shown that British-controlled financial secrecy jurisdictions and British law are used by dictators, oligarchs, drug barons, corporations and billionaires to launder and accumulate illicit money, fuelling poverty, war, and injustice around the world.[6] Yet while we in the UK pride ourselves on a culture that does not tolerate corruption—interests have to be declared, judges are not open to bribes—the measures introduced thus far to remedy the UK's facilitation of global corruption are so limited they amount to little more than window-dressing.

There is a specifically modern form of invisible violence in the way that even the rhetoric of transparency is used to obfuscate facts. In the modern technological world interest-groups can blind with science; and legislation—for example in highly specialist areas of trade and patenting that directly affect the lives of millions—can be rendered almost impenetrable through 'salami-slicing' technicalities. Horrific evils seem remote from most of us in the developed world, as has been mentioned above. Not only are we often the beneficiaries of evil (for instance through scandalously cheap clothing and food) and thus have every disincentive to challenge them, but their visible manifestations such as collapsed factories and polluted oceans do not immediately impact on us. We lack an effective public language of moral urgency.

---

[6] For example, see the FinCEN Files investigation undertaken by the International Consortium of Investigative Journalists, September 2020. https://www.icij.org/investigations/fincen-files/what-is-the-fincen-files-investigation/ (accessed 14 May 2021).

## *Language that distances us from reality*

Biblical imagery drew from familiar physical realities. Even the visions of *Revelation* had immediate physical reference: seals, horsemen, swords, crowns, disease-raddled bodies were not just figurative, though we in affluent societies cannot be reminded too often that destitution, killer metalware, and militarist swagger are still all too real worldwide. Those in the city of Ephesus who were exhorted to put on the armour of God would probably at least occasionally have seen armoured soldiery. Armour represented an entirely real physical authority. Now, for most of us in the developed world, such images—and indeed the cross and much of the central vocabulary of Scripture—have almost completely lost their literal dimension. Ancient weaponry, monarchs, and symbols survive, sometimes in futuristic versions of themselves, as props in fantasy games and movies. But like modern currencies, they are no longer anchored in gold-standard tangible reality. Vital Christian images like the shepherd, sowing and reaping, and blood sacrifice are purely literary. We lack imagery that relates to our lives in the way New Testament writings related to the ordinary life of people in first-century Palestine. Our spiritual language and mind-set are thus in many ways unconsciously historicist, making perfect sense in their own self-enclosed terms but disengaged from the world around us.

The word 'evil' is compromized to the extent that it is associated with this historicist, movie- and game-world mindset. And this in turn impacts on our ability to identify the specifically spiritual nature of evil in its modern guises, whether in mainstream media or on the dark web, or in the financial instruments of corporate tax avoidance and the erosion of accountability through commercial confidentiality, labyrinthine sub-contracts, and small-print exemptions. The distinction between crime and sin has little leverage in a society that can evaporate corruption into incentives, management fees, and loans. Swords and ploughshares have little purchase in a world of nuclear weapons, cyber attacks, disinformation, and corporate agribusiness. Activists and documentary-makers have managed to generate the beginnings of a political response to the climate crisis, where traditional religious language of praise for creation failed over decades to prevent devastating ecological abuse. But even now environmental arguments have to speak of the financial value of nature. 'Alternative' spiritualities have attempted to meet a sensed lack of meaningful speech and action, but remain marginalized. The cunning of serpents and innocence of doves are required, along with a formidable amount of hard factual information, if a genuinely effective spiritually dissenting voice is to be heard in a crisis-driven world.

## The Christian imperative to engage

Some Christians argue that identification of and resistance to evil is essentially a matter of inner personal engagement. Indeed, 'doing good' or trying to be 'relevant' to our own age are sometimes derided as superficial, merely ethical not spiritual. Yet while Christ often withdrew to pray, he also personally confronted the hypocrisy and abuse of power in his own day, and his teaching demonstrates that a faith not substantiated in neighbourly *caritas* is without substance, indeed is damnable (Matt. 25). Insofar as we are called to imitate Christ and to help those in need—not just reactively being 'neighbour' to those who fall among thieves but also, empowered by the Holy Spirit, asking, 'Why are the poor poor?', championing justice as well as practising compassion—it is incumbent upon us to articulate our understanding of evil both within ourselves and in the world around us, and to act upon that understanding.

I have talked about the fascination of obvious evil and our propensity for judgementalism, often based on class or 'otherness'. Noting that speech is just part of how we come to awareness and how we communicate, I have talked about the 'languages' of marketing, violence, and fear, and about the disjunction of spiritual and ethical discourses, as well as problems within our traditional spiritual vocabulary. I have alluded to the disembodied sphere of activity of good and evil created by the internet, and the huge complexity of a social contract ever more dependent on specialist legal negotiation at the expense of trust. How can we speak not merely clearly but effectively about good and evil, in a world where traditional moral and religious codes are declared relative, abusive, or lacking credibility, or are applied with new literalness and harshness?

## Virtue and the self

Most who seek to live a good life are no doubt well-intentioned. But we do not always acknowledge we can have mixed motives. Also that even some of our best intentions may inadvertently be paving the road to hell. A striking example of the way good ideas become distorted is the widespread invocation of Adam Smith to justify a form of capitalism of which it is impossible to imagine the eighteenth-century 'Father of Economics' would have approved.[7] Sharply differentiating self-interest from selfishness, Smith identified self-interest as the most reliable element of human psychology with regard to social and economic relationships. His analysis cut through much cant about noble aspirations, devotion to duty, and selfless virtue.[8] Yet in today's economic thinking self-interest is not merely that which motivates most human beings in most situations, it has become the ultimate virtue. The sole purpose of a company, a legal personality, is to make a profit. Our primary responsibility in a consumer society is to consume, and to better ourselves to earn enough to consume more. The 1980s slogan 'Greed is good' summed up a moral vision of *homo economicus* that even the committed monetarist Margaret Thatcher agreed was not how 'trickle-down' was meant to work. Mainstream economic theory now also speaks of the importance of amorphous factors such as well-being and even happiness. Yet it is difficult to see how in practice this is anything more than tempering of a system still based on individualistic self-interest

---

[7] Cf. Adam Smith, *The Theory of Moral Sentiments* (London: Cadell and Davies, 1812).

[8] Smith's distinction between self-interest and selfishness is discussed concisely by Lauren Hall at https://www.adamsmithworks.org/documents/self-interest-rightly-understood (accessed 14 May 2021).

and driven politically by a rhetoric of growth and financial GDP. Prime Minister Boris Johnson's recent remark to the parliamentary 1922 committee that, 'The reason we have the [COVID-19] vaccine success is because of capitalism, because of greed my friends',[9] exemplifies the continuing linguistic strategy of airbrushing evil by inverting it and presenting it as a social good. His comment, quickly retracted, was all the more shocking as development of the COVID vaccine was largely funded by the government (that is the taxpayer), precisely because of a *failure* of capitalism: pharmaceutical businesses being uninterested in investing in a one-off health solution that, unlike drugs for heart conditions, cancer, or depression would not yield steady ongoing profits

The process whereby a highly selfish form of self-interest became the default motor of social thinking, and has essentially remained so despite the 2007/8 financial crash, involved mutations in every sphere of professional, economic, business, and academic life. Values such as mutuality and loyalty ceded to the 'virtues' of a bonus culture, bottom-line efficiency, and competition at the expense of collaboration in everything from health to education. Even in mainstream psychology and the soft self-help industry, altruism is seen as suspect or outright damaging: traditional Christian talk of selflessness, it is claimed, has left people with low self-esteem; we must learn to love ourselves.

It is an indictment of traditional institutional Christianity that the self came to be seen as somehow implicitly evil. The language of the cross and self-denial only makes sense within a framework of unconditional and infinite love. Jesus teaches, 'love your neighbour as yourself'. What poor sort of love do we offer our neighbour if we neglect, despise, or abuse our 'self'? Right self-love is an offering of praise and thanks to God for that which we know more intimately — albeit still incompletely — than anything else in creation, namely the body and relational economy in which we exist. While the spectacular

---

9 *The Guardian* (24 March 2021) https://www.theguardian.com/politics/2021/mar/23/greed-and-capitalism-behind-jab-success-boris-johnson-tells-mps (accessed 14 May 2021).

austerities of Christian ascetics down the ages perhaps encouraged an attitude of 'contempt of the world' that involved hatred of the self, the great spiritual teachers have consistently warned against the evil of falling into such a self-harming spiritual trap. Language is crucial here. As the Carmelite nun Ruth Burrows observes in her book *Before the Living God* there is a vital distinction between the self and the ego. 'The self must triumph over the ego', over 'basic self-orientation'.[10] Contempt of self can be a thing of the ego. 'But it is precisely our nature to go beyond the limits of our nature so as to enter into God!' The current secular convention of 'love yourself' is understandable as a corrective to damaging, supposedly Christian incitements to self-loathing. Yet it accords all too ominously with an ego-based culture of retail therapy and ad-driven consumerism that directly clashes with values we profess to care about. Our love of freedom and choice is afflicted with spiritual double-think, a modern manifestation of *dipsychia* (Jas 1:8) in which we want to be seen to have fine values while also enjoying the cheap luxuries of consumer culture. We have extraordinary means to live well, and extraordinary means to fail to see, or to forget, the cost to others and to the planet.

## A higher language

The law, theology and philosophy, science and technology, commerce, the arts all offer tools with which to pursue good and address evil. Yet out of them breed venal legalism, pretentiousness, career-skewed science, dehumanizing managerialism, and novelty aping creativity. The only power able to break this bondage to self-magnification and untruth is that of hope and love, learned through the Word that is 'the way and the truth and the life' (John 14:6).

Hope and love disconnected from actions that give them meaning remain, however, in the realm of Simone Weil's 'imaginary good'.

---

[10] Ruth Burrows, *Before the Living God* (London: Burns and Oates, 2008). Quoted in Philip Harvey's very thoughtful selection https://thecarmeliteli-brary.blogspot.com/2018/04/ten-quotes-from-ruth-burrows.html (accessed 14 May 2021).

Preachy answers to real, intractable, agonizing issues are 'boring'. Equally, secular society finds 'doing good' boring—unless of course colour-heightened with the stardust of saintliness or personal failings/tragedies that hitch onto our desire for what Weil calls 'romantic and varied'.

What then is 'real good'?

## Evil and self-understanding

The failure to see that 'real good is always new, marvellous, intoxicating' derives not only from the positive inclination of evil toward the sensational, the facile, the self-pampering, but also from its negative nature as parasitic upon the good. This Augustinian conception is disputed, and across Western society today probably more dualistic views prevail. But from his Manichaean days Augustine would have understood the appeal of vehicles of modern dualism such as the Jungian 'shadow' or Western versions of Yin/Yang holism. His vision of *privatio boni* was a remarkable affirmation of goodness and challenge to despair in a world whose historic central pillar had collapsed with the sack of Rome in 410 AD.

Augustine's language of faith, hope, and love was not merely cerebral. It spoke also through his practical, political, and pastoral work as a bishop. Unlike marketing language, which promotes an aspirational image of a current product, he sought, especially in *The City of God,* real, eternally valid solutions to existential crises. And he brought to it not lofty expertise, but the humanity of his flawed self. In his *Confessions* his ashamed recollection of teenage sexual bravado famously veers into a yet more intensely painful memory of banal vandalism, when he and his 'gang' shook the pears from a laden pear tree for the sheer pleasure of wrong-doing. He interrogates how, as a young man with a potentially stellar career ahead, but more importantly a beloved child of God, he could debase himself to such destructive pettiness. The emotional heat of the writing communicates a lived experience of torturing self-analysis that is still powerful to read.

This writing about evil was, for me, in exhilarating contrast to the ideal of dispassionate observation I had been brought up to admire. Yet the two are mutually indispensable. Some critics see Augustine's pear tree confession as self-flagellation over an adolescent peccadillo. And there will always be readers unable to read between the lines of factual reporting, or who claim that because absolute objectivity is impossible there is no such thing as fact. The kingdom of the Father of Lies, however, is a protean void ('gloomy, monotonous, barren, boring' as Simone Weil has it) having no substance in itself, identifiable only through its infinite manifestations in human experience and reflection.

In the Lord's Prayer, 'evil', *tou ponerou*, might be better translated as 'the evil one'. Evil is not an abstract force. Though stronger than us (cf. St Paul's 'what I hate I do', Rom. 7:15) it is on our level, it has no more than creaturely substance. It lacks the ultimate reality, inexpressible in purely human terms, of the good. Dante, encountering our *'padre antico'*, Adam, in Canto 26 of *Paradiso*, sees only movement in the radiance of grace, like the wriggling of an animal in a sack.[11] The physicality of the image is astounding. Inversely, we similarly know evil through its motion in the 'sack' of human experience: its blockage, inflation, and destruction of feelings, imaginative vision, empirical reality, creaturely action, and order.

Speech is part of this 'sack' of human being, inseparable from seeing and hearing, which in turn are inseparable from thinking, feeling, and doing. Moreover the individual is inseparable from wider humanity, we have a shared identity in which peer actions and perceptions are decisive. Augustine, recalling the plan to despoil the pear tree, refers to such peer pressure: 'As soon as the words are spoken, "Let's go, let's do it", we are ashamed not to be shameless'[12]—and his confession is in a way itself a response to a higher, redemptive

---

[11] From Robin Kirkpatrick's translation of *The Divine Comedy*, Penguin Classics (London: Penguin, 2012).

[12] Augustine, *Confessions*, Book II, chapter 9, English version in Henry Chadwick, trans., *Saint Augustine: Confessions*, Oxford World's Classics (Oxford: OUP, 2008), 34.

'peer pressure', an *imitatio Christi* through which he seeks to conform his whole being ever more completely to Christ.

The wriggling of evil, futility, vanity, nothingness within human consciousness and sensory experience is entirely comprehensible to the mind's eye. It excites and satisfies because it is at our own ontic level. We can grasp it. By contrast the Christian *summum bonum* is beyond comprehension or imaginative apprehension. Systematic theology can at best demonstrate its ineffability, while at the sensory level 'good morals make bad art': Milton's Satan, as Daniel Lloyd finds above, is 'miserable, inspiring revulsion and pity', but the relative insipidness of his 'goodies' is also notorious; Dante's *Inferno* is read more than his *Paradiso*.[13] Only in mystical writing, through negatives, paradoxes, and startling shifts of register like the wriggling of Adam, does the language of goodness start to become humanly compelling.

## Good revealed through manifestation of evil

Unlike superficial fascination with evil, serious presentations of evil affirm the good by a kind of double negative, portraying a destructive force having only negative reality. Dante's Hell is an expression of Divine justice. Herman Melville said of Moby Dick 'I have written a wicked book, and feel spotless as the lamb'.[14] His wickedness magnifies the Lord: the whale symbolizes 'a colourless, all-colour of atheism from which we shrink'.[15] The biblical story of the Fall is a 'dramatic device' for an epic—*felix culpa*—of the love of God.

Simone Weil sees through the 'imaginary' of evil because she has an essentially mystical vision of the good. Similarly, whereas a modern writer might dwell on the young Augustine's sex life, the

---

[13] See above, Daniel Lloyd, pages 18–20.

[14] Herman Melville, letter to Nathaniel Hawthorne, November 1851, http://www.melville.org/letter7.htm (accessed 14 May 2021).

[15] Herman Melville, *Moby Dick* (London: Richard Bentley, 1851), chapter 42, 'The Whiteness of the Whale'. The chapter is a vast, astonishing accumulation of images and reflections of pallor and whiteness in the world, of all of which 'the Albino whale was the symbol'.

saint himself sees the implications of intent, and of acts such as the abandonment of his 'concubine' for a socially advantageous marriage, that his world accepted as normal and thus not evil.

As already indicated, however, our vision of the good is only realisable through that to which we can relate as fallen creatures within the 'sack' of our creaturely economy. No creature can look on God and live (Ex. 33:20). Glory thus comes veiled … in wine (John 2.11), miraculous healing, loving fellowship. And in conflict, cruelty, and death: immanent in creation, glory transcends categories of human distinction.

This glory, that 'darkness' cannot comprehend, is unveiled in Christ, the Word of love. Yet in our fallen condition we realize love most comprehensively only through what endangers and appears to destroy it. The language by which ultimate goodness is known and hence evil unmasked is a mystery, not subject to any univocal human grammar. It is spoken cataphatically in the life and teaching of Jesus, and apophatically in the evil drawn out and exposed through the violence he endures. We speak truly of evil only when we hear and respond to the 'great cry' of the Word from the cross, acknowledging the transcendent glory of matter as Christ bows His head and surrenders His spirit, and realizing through our own discipleship of love what has been 'accomplished'.

## Pentecost and the redemption of speech

Whether we speak confrontationally or discreetly about evil; whether we preach confident in salvation, proclaiming the sins we have been forgiven; whether we speak with understanding, hesitant to imply we are better than others; or whether, motivated by kindness or piety, fear or complicity, we attempt to stay silent, to 'speak no evil': in the end evil will infiltrate human strategies, rhetorical or silent. The language it cannot endure is that of a heart actively attentive to the Word and a life shaped by the teaching of the Word. Incarnate, no abstract concept or moral code, the ethic and spirituality of the Logos are miraculously one.

Yet all verbal expression, even inspired Scripture, is a tent of non-miraculous human conventions. The tent-tabernacle of flesh in which the Word has pitched among us is provisional: perishable and open to misunderstanding, because truly human. At the same time, however, we claim in Trinitarian faith that this provisionality is, in a manner beyond human comprehension, itself taken up into the economy of the eternal. Like Mary in the garden and Thomas in the upper room, we are called to engage with a goodness beyond our instinctive desire to touch, preserve, and own. It is by openness to an incomprehensible other dimension of humanity within the ordinary condition of human living, the risen Christ among us, that we confess the good. And it is as we descend with no claim upon evidential truth from the mount of Ascension that we forge the language of discipleship wherein evil can be confronted.

We should indeed 'speak no evil', but evil can be eloquent by our silence. We speak no evil only when we positively speak the Way that is Truth and Life. Only when we lower the monkey paws that censor what we wish not to acknowledge, and open our hearts to the purging and anointing of the Holy Spirit, are we 'understanded' in the marketplace and able to communicate the Word. A Word spoken not only or perhaps even primarily through religious discourse and institutions, but through the mystery of the Church as only God knows it to be, the glorious company of the faithful and of those who by their actions and self-giving love reflect in this aeon of darkness 'the light of the world'.

—◆—

# PRAYER
## AND THE STRUGGLE AGAINST EVIL

## Alexander Ryrie

SOME YEARS AGO I had a conversation with a bishop of the Orthodox Church in Greece, during which I asked about the state of the church in his country. After a long pause he said simply,

'Struggling'.

Thinking that he was probably referring to practical difficulties such as shortage of priests or money, or people deserting the church, I asked, 'Struggling against what?'

He replied with just the one word, 'Evil'.

'And where is the evil?', I asked

'In people and in situations.'

I was left reflecting about the question of evil. How does it get into 'people and situations'? What can we do to contend with it? And is it the task of the church to struggle against evil?

This essay is one result of that reflection.

## 'In people and in situations'

None of us needs to be reminded that terrible situations exist and horrific events happen in the world around us. We need only open our newspapers or turn on our televisions to hear of war and violence, situations of injustice and oppression, acts of crime or terrorism. When we are confronted by such things, the word 'evil' comes readily to our lips. We sense that events and situations of this kind are not just unfortunate and regrettable: they have a different character that we can only describe as evil. Such evil deeds and situations have been a part of human life throughout history, and we seem to be unable to do anything about them.

What then is this thing we call 'evil'? In talking of evil, I am not thinking of something that is mainly encountered in weird occult practices, but of something that is more subtly mysterious, more all-pervasive and more obviously destructive than that. Just what evil is, how it comes about and why it exists, is a question that philosophers and theologians have wrestled with for centuries without reaching any clear answers. Evil is a mystery that we cannot account for, explain or understand; but that does not mean it does not exist.

The way in which something that we call evil erupts unexpectedly, inexplicably and uncontrollably in human societies and individuals, spoiling lives and creating misery and chaos, suggests that it is objectively real, something that does not arise only from the intention of a few wicked people, but which exists independently, as some kind of mysterious and malevolent power. The fictional depictions described above by Daniel Lloyd arise from a deep realisation that evil is all around and the horror genre frightens us precisely because it is based on reality. There seems to be something which stalks, subverts and corrupts the life of the world, a 'shapeless horror that threatens human life'. 'Human life', says John Barton, 'is distorted and corrupted by forces that human beings cannot control'.[1] The reality of evil 'in people and in situations' presses upon

---

[1] See above, John Barton, page 3.

us. It works in hidden, stealthy ways, entering and affecting human life often where it is least expected, and subverting our efforts for good. On the level of human history, the most idealistic enterprises get spoiled by envy and love of power; revolutionary movements to overcome injustice and oppression become new forms of tyranny; religious fervour turns to bigotry and hatred; and the attempt to build a world of freedom, justice and plenty for all is constantly frustrated by hidden obstacles. On the personal level, attempts to make ourselves into better people frequently end in frustration; our virtues tend to make us self-righteous, and our best intentions are compromised by hidden selfish motives. Of course, human life at the individual and the corporate level is also characterized by kindness, caring, courage and generous self-sacrifice. Yet these are often subverted and undermined by what seems like a hidden force that prevents humanity from overcoming the deep flaws in its individual and corporate life.

Evil then is an objective reality, but of a non-material or spiritual kind. As a spiritual reality it penetrates into every corner of human mental and social life. It is there not only in human deeds but in people's thoughts, feelings and motives, and in their relationships. That is not to say that human beings are evil through and through. Being made in the image of God, they are not basically or fundamentally wicked. If there is evidence of evil in the world and in human beings, there is also evidence of great goodness, splendid magnanimity and costly self-sacrifice. Although evil can take people over and incline them towards wicked ways, it is not inherent in human nature. 'Wickedness', says Paul Ricœur, 'is not something that replaces the goodness of a man; it is the staining, the darkening, the disfiguring of an innocence, a light and a beauty that remain'.[2] Evil is, nevertheless, inextricably interwoven into human life, so that we do not seem to be able to escape from it or avoid it.

In spite of this, 'evil' is not a word that we come across very often in the formal language of the church today. It is true that every

---

[2] Paul Ricœur, *The Symbolism of Evil* (New York: Harper and Row, 1967), 156.

time we say the Lord's Prayer we ask God to 'Deliver us from evil', but our liturgies, prayers and sermons, while making frequent reference to 'sins' or 'sin', make very little reference to evil.[3] We do not usually think of the church as engaged with a struggle against evil, as the Greek bishop did. 'Sin' is increasingly used a euphemism for evil as if 'evil' is a word that is too difficult, alarming or dangerous to state explicitly.

The Bible, however, has a lot to say about evil. Some important parts of the Bible, such as the Synoptic Gospels and the Psalms, refer more frequently to 'evil' than they do to 'sin' or 'sins'. And here too evil is assumed to be an objective reality. It is referred to or described by various words and metaphors, and by the use of a number of different myths or mythical concepts. Sometimes, particularly in the Gospels, evil is thought of as a personal reality—the 'devil' or the 'evil one'. Elsewhere in the New Testament it is described in terms of a variety of spiritual forces, such as 'principalities and powers', (or 'rulers and authorities'), the classic place being in the letter to the Ephesians:

> For our struggle is not against enemies of blood and flesh, but against the rulers, against the authorities, against the cosmic powers of this present darkness, against the spiritual forces of evil in the heavenly places (Eph. 6:12., see also 2 Col. 1:5).

For Paul and his associates evil was something cosmic, a kind of superhuman force working through a variety of spiritual agencies, affecting and corrupting human life. Something similar can be said of some of the Old Testament writers, who attempt to portray evil sometimes by using stories of a mythical type, as in Genesis 3, or by implicit reference to the ancient Near-Eastern myths of the overcoming of primeval chaos in the form of a dragon or sea monster,

---

[3] For example, during a celebration of the Eucharist according to the liturgy of the Church of England's *Common Worship*, the word 'sin' will occur in one form or another at least ten times, but the word 'evil' only once: during the Lord's Prayer.

as in the Psalms or Isaiah.[4] The Bible makes it clear that, although evil is inexplicable and mysterious, something that can be described only by symbol, metaphor and myth, it is nevertheless a powerful and objective reality that seeks to reduce human life to chaos and to separate human beings from their true life in God. The biblical belief, of course, is that God is more powerful than evil, and that in Christ He has won the victory over it and 'disarmed the principalities and powers'. But that does not mean that evil no longer exists. The enemies, wild beasts, dragons and waters of chaos that symbolize evil in the Psalms are with us still. The 'spiritual forces of evil' are still at large in the world, creating havoc and dragging humanity downwards.

## The struggle with evil

What then can we do about it? The answer given by the Bible and Christian tradition is that we should *struggle with evil*. The passage from Ephesians quoted above (and which we will examine more closely below) begins with the exhortation to 'put on the armour of God' because 'our struggle is not against enemies of flesh and blood, but against ... the spiritual forces of evil'; and it goes on to paint a picture of the Christian soldier armed to fight against evil. Following this, Christian writers and preachers, from the time of the early Fathers to our own day, have urged the need to engage in this struggle. The Desert Fathers saw themselves as engaging in a constant battle against evil in the form of demons. The theme of 'spiritual

---

[4] Explicitly in Ps. 74:13–14; 89:9–10; Is. 51:9–10, and implicitly elsewhere. In my study of the Psalms, *Deliver us from Evil: Reading the Psalms as Poetry* (London: Darton Longman & Todd, 2005), I suggest that not only the poetic images of wild beasts, of the great waters and the deep, of snares, traps and nets, and of bondage, imprisonment and separation, but also the 'enemies' and the 'nations' referred to very frequently, should be read as symbols and metaphors describing the reality and power of evil in a way which cannot adequately be done in rational prose. It is worth noting that there is no mention of a personal devil in the Old Testament.

warfare' was taken up by other early Fathers, and has been continued, particularly in the Christian East. Hymns that are still sung in our churches today speak of Christian soldiers fighting the battles of the Lord. We may not always like the military metaphors and some of the triumphalist sentiments, but the idea of spiritual warfare lives on. So long as evil exists in the world, Christians feel themselves called to do battle with it. As the Greek bishop said, the church is involved in a struggle against evil 'in people and in situations'.

How is this done? How, in practice, do we engage in a struggle against evil? If evil is a power beyond human control, what can we do to fight against it? We can try to fight it in a number of ways: one way is to attempt to mitigate the effects of evil on people's lives. By political and personal means we can work to remove or reduce injustices, wars, crimes, and needless human suffering, and there is no doubt that much can be achieved in this way, especially by dedicated, sacrificial and sustained effort. But there is also ample evidence that efforts of this kind, valuable and necessary though they are, do not remove evil or destroy its power. They can be very beneficial in mitigating the effects, but they disengage with the reality of evil. This reality is spiritual, and the struggle against evil is essentially a spiritual one. It must involve spiritual methods, principally the method of prayer.

There is more than one way of engaging with evil through prayer. One way is simply to cry to God against it. It is significant that the Lord's Prayer, the special prayer of the church, culminates with the petition 'Deliver us from evil'. A prayer that the world and individual human people may be saved from the power of evil is a central part of Christian spirituality. A concern about evil in the world makes us take this prayer with the utmost seriousness. Using this petition we can acknowledge and face the evil that surrounds us and call to God to rescue us from it. To 'cry to Him day and night' (Luke 18:7) against the injustices and cruelties that afflict people and the forces of evil that penetrate within us, is part of the Christian vocation.

Another way is to pray for the perpetrators of evil deeds. It is significant that there is only one place in the Gospels where Jesus tells us to pray for particular kinds of people, and this is when He said, 'Love your enemies and pray for those who persecute you' (Matt. 5:44). And we know that He followed His own precept when He prayed for those who crucified Him (Luke 23:34). To pray for the enemies of society, those who oppress others, who commit crimes of violence, who misuse power for their own ends and who cause the innocent to suffer, should be a part of the prayer of Christian people. In our corporate and individual prayers we rightly pay a lot of attention to praying for the victims of evil, those who suffer because of the cruelty and selfishness of others. In the name of Christ we need to pray also for those through whom such evil erupts in the life of the world. One of the Desert Fathers said, 'If a man wants God to hear his prayer quickly, then before he prays for anything else ... he must pray with all his heart for his enemies.'[5] Christian prayer must include prayer with all our heart for the enemies of society and of innocent people.

The struggle against evil involves something more, something deeper and more personal. This is because evil is not just something external that affects the lives of other people, but something *within* us. Although it apparently exists independently of human beings, it operates in and through them. It does not require very much thought to recognize that violence, vicious crimes, acts of cruelty, regimes of oppression and institutions of injustice all have their origin in the thoughts, feelings, desires, attitudes and prejudices that exist or arise within people. Certainly, evil seems to operate on a transpersonal level as well. It exists within the structures of society and the network of human relationships—'in situations'—in such a way that individual people can get caught up in something evil that is bigger than themselves, as James Ramsay has discussed above. The ultimate basis or location of evil, however, and the base of its operations, is the human heart. It is from the heart that there arise not only major and terrible acts of violence, and the injustice and oppression that characterize much of human life, but also the individual crimes of theft

---

[5] Zeno 7, in Sr Benedicta Ward SLG, *The Sayings of the Desert Fathers: The Aphabetical Collection*, Cistercian Studies, 59 (London: Mowbray, 1975), 67.

and murder, and the personal vices of avarice, wickedness, deceit, licentiousness, envy, slander, pride, folly. In the words of Jesus, 'all these evil things come from within' (Mark 7:22–3).

If this is true it implicates us all. If evil lodges in the heart, it lodges in everyone. The evil of the world is *our* evil, not simply that of other people. It operates in the hearts not only of a certain number of particularly wicked individuals, but of all. The feelings and motives that lie at the base of terrible deeds are to be found, to some degree, in all human beings. While it is obvious that there are some people who carry out particularly evil deeds, people through whom evil seems to erupt in tangible ways in human life, there can be no doubt that evil is located not only in them but in everyone. Those of us who do no obviously-evil deeds, who are not guilty of any crimes or serious misdemeanours, nevertheless have the seeds of evil within us. If we do not carry out acts of evil, we may still be harbouring it. In the case of some diseases, even people who have no symptoms and in whom the disease has not burst out, can still be 'carriers', people who appear to be free of it, but in whom the disease is present in a way that is sometimes hard to detect. It is something like this with evil: it may not be obvious—just a stumbling block—but if we think it is not there, 'we deceive ourselves' (1 John 1:8). We cannot truthfully pretend that the avarice, deceit, envy, and pride and other emotions that give rise to situations of evil exist only in other people.

If, then, we are seriously going to struggle against evil we need to start with ourselves, acknowledging and accepting that we are in part responsible for what goes on in the world around us. To believe that evil can be dealt with simply by punishing, reforming or getting rid of a certain number of evil people, or only by eradicating the social causes of violence and crime, without acknowledging that it lies within each of us, is a dangerous error of self-deception—and it is largely by deception that evil exists in people. By its insidious and subtle operation in the heart, it constantly seduces us into believing that the wrong lies in others and not in us.

## The passions

Since evil has its base of operations in the heart, the struggle against it is one that takes place deep within us. How do we engage in this inner struggle? We need first to understand what is meant by the word 'heart'. Used in the biblical sense, it refers not simply to our feelings or emotions, but to our whole inner self; the inner core of our personality, our deepest and most essential self, the seat and mainspring of our thoughts and feelings. The heart is our essential self, the place where we know ourselves to be 'me', the inner secret centre of ourselves into which no one else can come. It is here, in this secret, inner place that evil finds its base, its centre of operations. It is from here that evil actions spring. And so the struggle against it must take place within this hidden inner place within us.

The way that evil operates within our hearts is through what the early Fathers called the 'passions'. By this they meant, not some extreme of 'passionate' feelings, not only strong feelings of anger or desire, but all those emotional urges and ingrained subjective attitudes that deflect people from their relationship with God, and prevent them from being their true and best selves. There were various lists of the passions, but generally they included these eight: gluttony, lust, avarice, *acedia* or apathy, anger, despair, vainglory and pride. This list may seem artificial and unreal to some of us today, but it was based on the experience of people of prayer and spiritual depth who had examined themselves and acknowledged the truth of what they discovered. The 'passions' described the negative things that they found within their hearts. If we are to understand the workings of evil within our hearts and struggle against it, we do not need to adopt the list of passions of the early Fathers but, following their example, we need to look deep within ourselves to discover our own 'passions': the kinds of feelings, motives and attitudes that are found within us, which influence and perhaps dictate our actions, and which come between us and God.

In doing so it is important to recognize that people differ one from another. Perhaps the early Fathers were too prescriptive, and assumed too readily that the same passions were found in greater or lesser measure in everyone. To us it is more obvious that people's inner experiences differ; that we have different emotional needs from one another and are motivated in different ways. Perhaps we need each to discover our passions for ourselves. What I present below is a modern version of the passions, and I expand them to nine items. This is an outline of an inner world that may not be relevant for everybody. Others might draw up a different list or describe the passions differently, in the light of their own experience. Nevertheless this list and description will, I believe, be recognized by some, and may provide an example of how passions can operate. This in turn will lead to a way of understanding what it means to struggle against evil.

According to this view, the passions can be divided into two groups: those that operate to boost our self-esteem and make us feel more self-sufficient, self-reliant and less in need of God; and those that come about when those in the first group fail to work. Many of them correspond to the passions described by the early Fathers, but they are not necessarily the same, and they are arranged differently.

In the first group I identify five passions. First comes *the desire to possess*. This is the grasping attitude, the urge to get what we can for ourselves, the wish to be able to own and exploit the world for our own advantage, the desire to seize our life and the things of this world and make them entirely our own. It is not a matter simply of owning possessions, but of being attached to them and deriving our life from them. It is the desire to have things, not simply so that we can enjoy them with thankfulness, but because we need them to make us feel better about ourselves, give us a sense of security, and boost our self-esteem. Second, along with the desire to possess goes something more subtle, *the desire to control*: the desire to be in charge of what happens to us, thus closing off the potential of the unforeseen. We would like to be able to control other people and what they say and do to us, so that we can have our own way and not be hurt or disaffected by other people's behaviour. We would like to be able to control events in so far as they affect us, so that we can feel that we are in charge. If we are in control we feel more secure, more confident in ourselves, less anxious about what might happen to us. And we use a great variety of subtle means, great and small, some of them quite unconscious, to try to control the people we relate to and the events of our life. Third, there is the *urge to gratify* our senses in an excessive way, to over-indulge in physical pleasures, perhaps to compensate for, or disguise from ourselves, our inner feelings of inadequacy or unease.

Then there are two closely related attitudes. One is what is usually called *pride,* but it is basically a matter of superiority—regarding ourselves as being, in one way or another, better than other people. This again can be very subtle, and can be hidden even from ourselves. It can go along with an apparent humility or meekness, and need not appear as outward arrogance. We are constantly tempted to make ourselves feel better by putting others down, sometimes by little things we say, often only in our secret thoughts. The other is what in old-fashioned language is called *vainglory.* This is *the love of our own reputation,* the wish to be praised and admired. When others say good things about us, think well of us and admire us, this perhaps does more than anything else to boost ourselves in our own eyes. So we are subtly tempted to manipulate other people so that we receive their praise or win their admiration.

These five 'passions' are ways in which we inwardly promote or advance ourselves, so that we can rely on ourselves and feel self-sufficient. If they succeed, we can feel masters of ourselves and our own lives, and we have little need for God. But they do not always work. They do not always give us security, peace and self-satisfaction.

The second group of four 'passions' are feelings that arise, or attitudes we adopt, when our inner attempts to promote or uphold ourselves through the first group of passions do not succeed: the first of these is *resentment* or bitterness, which is a form of anger. Let down by other people or by events, we feel inwardly angry and so become bitter or resentful. This too can be subtle and insidious. Acute resentment can turn into a deep-seated hatred. It is sometimes hidden and disguised even from ourselves, and our anger or ill-feeling becomes misdirected towards others, perhaps without our realizing it. Along with resentment, there can be *envy*, a feeling of sadness or bitterness that we do not have the abilities, achievements, reputation or possessions that other people have, a feeling that can be tiny and scarcely recognized, but can also become a major consuming emotion. Next there is *dispiritedness* or discouragement, corresponding to the 'depressions' and 'despair' mentioned in the early Fathers' lists. This takes many forms, from a simple 'can't-be-bothered-ness', to the listlessness implied in the word 'accidie' (spiritual or mental sloth or apathy), to a feeling of our own worthlessness, to deep depression, despair or nihilism. Finally, there is *anxiety*, one of the most prevalent and corrosive of all feelings. Unable to put ourselves on top of the world and to guarantee our own security, we are anxious about what may happen to us. And, at a deeper level, we can become anxious about our inner selves, uncertain of our identity or our worth. Anxiety gnaws at our feeling of well-being and undermines our peace of mind.

These nine 'passions', five that are attempts to promote and establish ourselves, and four of that are the result of our inability to do so, will not describe the experience of everyone. There can, I am sure, be other lists, representing the experience of people of other temperaments and personalities. But this list will at least illustrate the kinds of feelings and attitudes that underlie much of what takes place on the surface of our lives.

Underneath all these feelings there is perhaps something else: the early Fathers recognized that the basis of all the passions was what in Greek they called *philautia*, or 'self-love'. This refers to what we may call the false love of self. There is, of course, a right and appropriate love of self; a proper valuing or esteem of ourselves; a recognition of our worth and dignity as human beings; a desire to make the best of the lives given us. But *philautia* is self-love in the sense of 'self-centredness that snatches the world away from God to annex it, making neighbours into things'. When we are dominated by *philautia* our self-interest takes over. 'There is no longer the Other, nor other people, only the absolute I.'[6] This self-love underlies all the

---

[6] This and the previous quotation are from O. Clément, *The Roots of Christian Mysticism* (London: New City, 1993), 134.

passions. It is this that makes us try to promote and establish ourselves and make ourselves secure, and that casts us down when we do not succeed. According to Maximus the Confessor, 'whoever has *philautia* has all the passions'.[7]

And yet there is something deeper and more basic still. In the words of Maximus again, 'the cause of this deviation [of the natural energies into destructive passions] is the hidden fear of death'.[8] Underlying even our love of self is fear—fear of non-being, of our own nothingness, of the great void beneath us into which we may sink. That is why the psalmists speak of Sheol or the Pit, of *tehom*, the unfathomable deep, and of the overwhelming waters. It is this fear of the great abyss of nothingness below us that makes us cling to ourselves, and prompts us to boost, support and attempt to sustain ourselves. It is this that casts us down into listlessness or despair and arouses our anxiety when our self-promotion lets us down. The 'passions', whatever form they may take, are all the outworkings of this basic existential fear that lurks within us, often hidden and unrecognized.

These 'passions' are the working of evil within us. It is the mysterious power of evil that in some strange way engenders passions such as these in the human heart, promotes *philautia*, and stirs up the fear of death, making people behave in ways that are hostile to others and inimical to their true selves, contributing to the evils of the world at large. It is the power of evil that makes us reach for a self-sufficiency that separates us from God. It is these feelings and attitudes that tend to spoil our lives by coming between us and God, and prevent us from being our true selves in freedom. In so far as we are governed or influenced by emotions arising from self-love and fear, we are not free to be the whole persons that God has made us to be.

It is not hard to recognize that it is these passions and the underlying self-love and fear that are the basic cause of the evils

---

[7] See O. Clément, *The Roots of Christian Mysticism*, 134.

[8] Maximus the Confessor, *Questions to Thalassios*, 61 (*Patrologia Graeca* 90,633), cited in Clément, *The Roots of Christian Mysticism*, 106 (the interpolation is Clément's), 135.

that erupt in the world. Wars, violence, exploitation and injustice, all have their roots precisely in these passions. The hatred and greed that distort human life are the tiny passions writ large. It is the existential fear and its resultant passions lurking in all of us that produce the terrible things that human beings do to one another. If we are to engage with the evil in the world, we need first and foremost to engage with the passions within ourselves. This may seem to be rather an extreme statement: many of our inner feelings and attitudes are apparently slight and trivial; little urges or petty thoughts of no significance. Moreover, to pay too much attention to them may seem over fastidious and nit-picking, a focus on mere peccadilloes. It is, of course, true that we can become obsessed with our own inner workings, over-concerned with our own trivial faults, so we need to guard against the struggle with evil turning into an obsession with ourselves. If we are seriously to engage with evil we need to attend to it at its root, that is, within the human heart. The struggle against evil is fundamentally a struggle with the passions, a struggle to free our feelings and attitudes from the distortions produced by self-love and fear.

## Resisting the passions

How, then, do we struggle against the passions and the evil that inspires them? The first and basic thing is to recognize and admit that we ourselves cannot overcome them. Human beings have wrestled with evil in various forms all through history, but have never overcome it. Evil is a power beyond our control. We believe, of course, that God has won the victory over evil through the death and resurrection of Christ; but evil still afflicts human life. The 'spiritual forces of evil' are still in the 'heavenly places' and we have to engage in the struggle against them, but the victory is in God's hands not ours.

We cannot overcome evil by ourselves but we can *resist* it. This is urged upon us in the New Testament, notably in the passage in Ephesians referred to above: 'Take up the whole armour of God, so

that you may be able to withstand [or 'resist'] on that evil day'
(Eph. 6:13); and also in the well-known verse of 1 Peter where in the
original the same Greek word is used:

> Be sober, be watchful. Your adversary the devil prowls around like
> a roaring lion, seeking someone to devour. Resist him, firm in your
> faith (1 Pet. 5:9).

What does it mean to resist evil, or the evil one? At the level of
our inner selves it involves at least two things: the first is being alert
and keeping watch. This idea, which is expressed by the use of three
different Greek words in the New Testament, is emphasized in these
same two passages from Ephesians and 1 Peter: 'Keep alert with all
perseverance', (Eph. 6:18); 'Be sober, be watchful', (1 Pet. 5:9). This
theme was taken up by the early Fathers who attached great importance to what they called *'nepsis'* (sobriety or alertness), and to
'guarding the heart'. To struggle against evil, they believed, it was
necessary to guard one's heart in order to try to prevent the passions
from entering. Evil operates in insidious and subtle ways, and it can
affect our feelings, motives and attitudes without our realizing it. So
it is important to be alert and ready to recognize the moments and
occasions when evil is creeping in.

Preventing the entry of evil is, once again, something we cannot
do for ourselves: for this we need the protection of God. We need,
as the letter to the Ephesians says, to 'put on the armour of God'.
This is followed in the epistle by a picture of the Christian as a soldier, protected by various pieces of amour and equipment: belt,
breastplate, shoes, shield, helmet and sword. What is important to
note is that each of these is a piece of the amour or protection supplied by God, not by ourselves. The armour is described as the belt
of *truth,* the breastplate of *righteousness,* the shoes of the gospel of
*peace,* the shield of *faith* or faithfulness, the helmet *of salvation,* and
the sword of the *Spirit.* All these words used to characterize the armour are common and important words in the Old Testament,
describing qualities or characteristics of God that He bestows as gifts
on His people. Each piece of protective equipment is something that

God gives us through His presence among and within us.[9] In the struggle against evil, and in order to prevent the entry of the passions, we need protection and help from beyond ourselves that is supplied by God himself. It is God alone, who by His truth, righteousness, peace, faithfulness, salvation and the working of His Spirit, provides our protection against evil. Struggling against evil in prayer involves calling to God to supply us with His armour by which alone we can resist or withstand.

## Acknowledge and offer

This resistance does not, however, totally rid us of evil, for we discover, sometimes by bitter experience, that the passions continue to affect us. We may have some success in reducing them, but if we think we have got rid of them we frequently find they return through the back door. Attempts to make oneself into a better, more moral and less selfish person may yield some useful results, but the hidden fear and the secret self-love tend to remain, disguised perhaps by a generous and caring exterior. The struggle against the passions seems to be an unequal combat, a battle we cannot win.

In this situation there are two more things that we can do. The first is simply to recognize and *acknowledge* our own passions. This is not as simple as it sounds, because they have a way of hiding themselves from our consciousness. Evil operates in the human heart in secret, subtle and insidious ways. Like the psalmists' deceitful and treacherous enemies, the wild beasts lurking in ambush or the hidden snares and traps that lay around them, the passions operate in hidden ways that we often do not recognize. Pride, resentment, the desire to control and all the others may be part of our feelings and attitudes without our realizing it, and may affect our behaviour secretly. Evil keeps its power partly by remaining hidden. One part of the struggle,

---

[9] Most of the phrases used in Ephesians to describe the armour are apparently taken from Isaiah 11:5 and 59:17; but the words 'truth', 'righteousness', 'peace', 'faithfulness', 'salvation' and 'Spirit' are key words used throughout the Old Testament to describe the character and activity of God.

therefore, consists of an honest and searching examination of our feelings and attitudes to discover the hidden passions. It involves acknowledging the hidden motives behind our actions, and facing our secret underlying fears. This can be a difficult and sometimes painful exercise, but the purpose of it is not simply to bring these things to our own awareness; rather, more importantly, it is to acknowledge them to God. Although we cannot hope by our own efforts to dispose of the passions, we can make a practice of bringing them up from the secret depths and laying them openly and honestly before God.

The second thing that goes along with acknowledging is *offering*. Having recognized something of the working of the passions within us, we can offer all of this to God. To offer is not simply to let go, but to hand over; to ask God to take and accept what we are bringing. Our inner feelings, attitudes and thoughts can all be offered to Him. This is done as part of our total self-giving, the complete offering of ourselves to God. We tend to think of offering God our good gifts, the best we have, and so it may seem strange to offer Him the workings of evil. However, the offering of our whole self involves everything, the good and the bad, and the offering of our passions is a part of this. We hand ourselves over to God just as we are, with all that is in us.

This offering of our passions as a part of our total self-offering is an essential element in our struggle against evil. This is because it links us with God's special work of overcoming evil, and provides a small opportunity for Him to act. God has His own way of dealing with evil, revealed and made effective supremely in the cross of Christ. He does so not by blasting it away,[10] but by transforming it through the process of costly self-offering. This is the mysterious work of God in Christ. When we offer ourselves and all that we are to Him, our offering is taken up into, and united with, the self-offering of Christ.[11] In this way

---

[10] A phrase used by J. D. Levenson in his thought-provoking book *Creation and the Persistence of Evil The Jewish Drana of Divine Omnipotence* (Princeton: Princeton University Press, 1988), xvii.

[11] This, of course, happens in a special way in the Eucharist, and is a part of the meaning and importance of the sacrament.

77

our little bit of the world's evil is laid before God for Him to transform. Our struggle to acknowledge and offer the passions at work within us is used by God in His work of overcoming evil.

Our struggle against evil, then, is not a striving for perfection or victory, it is a matter of acknowledging and offering; it involves an honest attempt to recognize and acknowledge our susceptibility to the passions, and to make that a part of the offering of our whole lives to God. These are the basic steps in the inner struggle against evil. Nor is it a matter of simply focussing on ourselves and our inner workings; it is not a self-centred obsession with ourselves. Through the process of acknowledging our passions and handing them over to God we open our inner selves to the working of God, and so involve Him in the struggle. This is more demanding than it may seem. Our natural tendency is to cover things up within ourselves and to leave them as they are. To acknowledge our inner state and offer it to God is to allow the possibility that the unforeseen may happen: that we may be transformed. To lay ourselves open in this fashion demands courage; it is a struggle, and this is the essence of our struggle against evil.

This struggle is, of course, an inner one, and an essential aspect of it is that it is carried out above all through *prayer*. It is in the course of prayer that the practice of acknowledging and offering is undertaken. It is before God that we search our hearts to discover our hidden passions. It is in His presence that we recognize them for what they are, and acknowledge that they are a part of us. And it is in the silence of our prayer that we hand all this over to God. Moreover, this requires prayer of a particular kind—the prayer of holding ourselves still before Him and being in His presence; the prayer of contemplation in which we wait for Him in silence.

Furthermore, engaging in silent prayer of this type leads us on to one more element crucial to the inner struggle against evil: having first of all examined ourselves before God and offered ourselves to Him, we then turn away from ourselves and focus on God alone, leaving everything to Him. In our waiting on God in silence we wrest our attention away from ourselves, trusting that God will deal with the passions that we have offered to Him, and direct our attention, our thoughts and our love entirely towards Him. He alone is our victory and our protection, and to turn our attention to Him and rest in Him is an essential part, and a supreme point, of our struggle.

## Deliverance from evil

Does this inner struggle with evil achieve anything? Does it deliver us from evil? And how does deliverance come about? The important thing to recognize here is that, although our struggle does not totally rid us of our passions or overcome the power of evil within us—let alone the tragic evils of the world—God uses it to lead us towards a situation in which we are delivered from evil. This situation is one characterized by two closely related things: *purity of heart* and a deeper *relationship* with God.

Purity of heart is an important biblical theme. The psalmist says that it is those who have clean hands and pure hearts who shall stand in God's holy place (Ps. 24:3–4). Purity of heart was a prerequisite for being in God's presence and for being in close and direct relation with Him. In this context the word 'pure' has a distinctive meaning. The Hebrew word used in Psalm 24:4 refers not to ritual purity, nor simply to the absence of immoral or unclean thoughts. It means pure in the sense of clear, simple and transparent, perhaps even shining; it is the state of our inner selves when our passions are overcome; it refers to singleness of mind, clarity of intention and will, and feelings centred not on ourselves but upon God, His ways and His gifts; it describes a heart that is luminous, limpid, transparent to the light of God, ready for His prompting, open to His workings within us.[12] This is impossible as long as our hearts are

---

[12] See Sebastian Brock, *The Syriac Fathers on Prayer and the Spiritual Life*, Cistercian Studies, 101 (Kalamazoo MI: Cistercian Publications, 1987), xxix ff., and *The Luminous Eye: The Spiritual World Vision of Saint Ephrem the Syrian*, Cistercian Studies, 124 (Kalamazoo MI: Cistercian Publications, 1992), 39f. This may be the meaning of the 'single' (*haplous*) eye of Matt. 6:22/Luke 11:34.

cluttered and clouded over with passions. It is when the heart is clear, transparent and limpid that we can see God. It is when our inner self is pure—that is to say unencumbered, uncluttered, single, and open, not taken over by other things, not chained to ourselves and to the need to promote, protect and establish ourselves—that we are able to 'ascend the hill of the Lord and stand in His holy place', and to have the close and intimate relationship in which we can 'see' Him.

This purity of heart is the gift of God, and it is given to us now only in small measure, if at all. As we acknowledge and hand over to God all that is in our hearts and call for His protective armour to enable us to resist, we open the way for God to do His work of purifying. When we offer up all the clutter within us He can begin to tidy up our overcrowded, confused and disordered hearts. God's work is done mainly in secret, and we may not be aware of it or see its results within us. We have probably all seen something of it in others, saintly men and women whose lives and whose whole being bear witness to the purity of their hearts; and we can trust that God will work to bring this about in us too.

It is through purity of heart that we are brought into a deeper relationship with God. Jesus said that the pure in heart would see God (Matt. 5:8). Seeing God is not simply an experience: it refers to a relationship. Seeing God means beholding His face, seeing Him face to face, and in the Bible the 'face' of God (the Hebrew *panîm*) refers to His presence. To see God is to come into His presence, to be with Him, in relationship with Him. In the vision of the book of Revelation, this will be the joy of the saints in heaven (Rev. 22:4). The pure in heart are not promised an ecstatic vision, but a deep close person-to-person relationship with God, summed up in the expression 'to see God's face'. This direct relationship is the ultimate goal of life, the fullest and most complete joy.

It is precisely this relationship with God that brings about ultimate deliverance from evil. Deliverance, or salvation, is not some external gift of God: it is simply God himself coming into relationship with us. When the psalmists cried out to God to deliver them, they were calling not for some gift to be given them, and not necessarily for some action on God's part, but simply for His presence. Evil for them was separation from God, and deliverance was God's overcoming of this separation by making himself present and being in relationship with them. When we say that 'Jesus saves', or speak of the salvation won for us by the death and resurrection of Christ, we mean nothing more nor less than that in this way we are brought into relationship with God. It is this relationship, and God's presence for us in it, that saves and delivers us from evil.

## The evil of the world

What about the evil around us, the horrors of war, injustice and crime that afflict the world that I mentioned at the start, and the insidious social normalization of wrongdoing described by James Ramsay above? How does our engagement with evil in the depths of ourselves have any effect on the evil in society? This happens in two ways. One is simply that, by acknowledging and offering our own 'passions' to God, we are made more truly into persons, and we thereby make the life around us a little bit more personal. One effect of the passions upon us is that they prevent us from being true persons. The feelings, thoughts and attitudes that make up our passions serve to promote and establish a false self, an image or idea of ourselves to which we have become attached, and that we must defend if we are not to be cast down and resentful. They are accretions that shroud our authentic selves. As our hearts are purified, these accretions are removed; the things that prevent us from being our true selves are taken away, and we can begin to be more authentic persons. We have less need to try to *be* someone or something, to build up and defend an image of ourselves. We can be content simply to be ourselves, the one basic, original, unique person that God has made us to be. As we enter into a deeper relationship with God we discover ourselves more fully as persons. Being enmeshed in evil has the opposite effect on us. Evil is sub-personal, or impersonal, something less than personal. It acts to separate us from God, and draw us away into a realm and a way of living that is not fully human.[13] However, because God is a 'person', we can address Him as 'Thou' or 'You', and enter into a personal 'I–Thou' relationship with Him. In doing so we discover our selfhood, and are affirmed as the persons we are. God is, of course, not a person in the human sense—He is not confined within the limits of human personhood—but He is certainly not *less* than a person. He may be thought of as 'supra-personal', the one absolute Person, from whom all personhood is derived. Martin Buber says, 'The concept of personhood is, of course, utterly incapable of describing the nature of God, but it is permitted and necessary to say that God is *also* a person.'[14]

When this happens we bring about a state of affairs in which human beings relate to one another as persons a little more closely. It is not difficult to recognize that many of the evils, wrongs, crimes and injustices in the world come about because, under the influence of our passions, we fail to regard others as persons, and we treat them impersonally as objects to be controlled and manipulated for our own ends. It is part of the aim of the impersonal and sub-human power of evil to make us treat one another in this way. When we all discover ourselves as persons in relation to God, and see our fellow humans as fellow persons, we will bring about a community of 'persons' in which evil will not thrive.

However, there is a more profound and more mysterious way in which our struggle with the evil-within-us affects the life of the world. If it is true that evil is a power beyond us, a spiritual reality whose principal place of working is within the human heart, then the struggle against it in the heart is part of the cosmic struggle against evil. It is an engagement with the power of evil in the place where it has its roots. To seek to eradicate it from the life of the world without paying attention to what is taking place in our own hearts is to avoid the essential struggle and to fall prey to evil's deceptions. By acknowledging and

---

[13] See John Barton above, page 2.

[14] Martin Buber, *I and Thou*, trans. W. Kaufmann, (Edinburgh: T. & T. Clark, 1970), 181.

offering what is happening within us, we are facing not only the evil within us but also the evil that, by its subtle deceptions, spreads its net over all of human life.

The struggle with evil, then, is essentially something that takes place in our inner selves, through prayer; through our continuous calling upon God to deliver us from evil; through our intercessions both for the victims and for the perpetrators of evil deeds; through our taking to ourselves the protection of God and guarding our hearts in watchfulness; through the rigorous searching of our hearts—our motives, attitudes and feelings—in His presence, and our laying all this before Him in the offering of our whole selves; and through our remaining still before Him in silent openness, trusting that He will give His gift of purity of heart and draw us into the deep relationship with Him in which we can see His face. Through this deep work of prayer we engage secretly and silently in a struggle with the evil both within us and around us. There is no more important task for Christian people today.

—◆—

# SLG PRESS PUBLICATIONS

**slgpress.co.uk**